# In His Hands

# In *His Hands*

A Mother's

Journey through

the Grief of

Sudden Loss

# Jenny Hess

Covenant Communications, Inc.

Cover image: *Heart-Shaped Rock in a Man's Hands* © Rosemarie Gearhart, courtesy of istockphoto.com

Cover design copyright © 2013 by Covenant Communications, Inc.

Author Photo courtesy of Carrie Maxfield

Published by Covenant Communications, Inc.
American Fork, Utah

Printed in the United States of America
First Printing: May 2013

19 18 17 16 15 14 13    10 9 8 7 6 5 4 3 2 1

ISBN 978-1-62108-251-4

For Kirk, who kept us adventurous
For Karissa, who brought music back into our lives
For Kyle, who kept us moving forward
For Jake, who kept us laughing
For Joey, who brought the magic back

And, of course,
For Russell, who connected us all to heaven

From me, the memory keeper

# Contents

Preface.................................................................xi

Acknowledgments.................................................xv

Chapter One: That Fateful Day...................................1

Chapter Two: The Day After.....................................23

Chapter Three: What Saved Me .................................29

Chapter Four: Living Together, Grieving Apart...............45

Chapter Five: More Precious than Gold.......................57

Chapter Six: Isolation ...........................................69

Chapter Seven: The Memory Quilt.............................75

Chapter Eight: Sorrow ..........................................81

Chapter Nine: Mother's Day....................................91

Chapter Ten: A Song of the Heart.............................97

Chapter Eleven: Russell Rocks.................................103

Chapter Twelve: Joseph Smith.................................107

Chapter Thirteen: Choices......................................113

Chapter Fourteen: Beauty for Ashes...........................119

Chapter Fifteen: Postraumatic Stress .........................139

Chapter Sixteen: Mind over Matter ...........................147

Chapter Seventeen: Surprised by Joy .........................149

Chapter Eighteen: The Debt....................................153

Chapter Nineteen: Why..........................................157

Chapter Twenty: Enough .......................................161

Chapter Twenty-One: Perspective.............................173

Chapter Twenty-Two: Gifts.....................................179

Chapter Twenty-Three: Looking Back.........................187

Epilogue...........................................................191

# *Preface*

I wanted to write this book to share with my family earlier experiences I had that prepared me for Russell's death, how others saved me after he died, and the many lessons I have learned through my grief. This story is not a tragedy, although it *is* sad. It is a piece of our history that one day will have a happy, eternal ending.

One day I told a friend about the day Russell died. I walked her through all the ways we felt the Lord had helped us. It may sound funny, but to me, Russell died in the best way possible. If he had to die—and we strongly feel that this was his time to go—this was the way that would leave the least amount of damage and pain to my other children and a way that would help to bind up our broken hearts later.

My friend told her mom my experience later that day, with the comment, "Isn't it nice that Heavenly Father prepared her that day for what she would have to go through?"

Her mom wisely but firmly answered, "Honey, Heavenly Father was preparing Jenny her *whole life* for this experience."

I have pondered that statement many times. In looking back on that day, we see the hand of the Lord gently guiding us. As I look further back through the weeks and months before Russell died, I see myself subtly being watched over, guided, and prepared. As I look back through the years—even before Russell was born and before Kirk and I were married—I see the hand of the Lord in my life, giving me experiences to teach me how to rely on Him. Although I had no idea that these experiences were preparing me and strengthening me for the horrifying experience of losing my son, it's because of these experiences that I'm able to survive this loss.

I had a companion on my mission who wrote in her journal in pencil. After a hard day, we would both furiously scrawl our deepest feelings,

feelings tinged with frustration and sometimes righteous indignation. The next morning, without fail, she would erase that page of her journal. I was aghast! How could she just disregard her thoughts, no matter how livid they might have been, and eradicate them so easily?

"I don't want to remember that painful experience," she explained. "And I don't want anyone else to ever know I felt like that."

I couldn't understand her then, but I feel that I do now. First, I didn't expect anyone to read my missionary journal, and maybe she didn't have the same expectation of privacy I enjoyed. And second, after writing about all that I've experienced and learned through Russell's death, I'm starting to appreciate that privacy. I am a private person. Throughout my life I have held my deepest, darkest, most painful and profound experiences close to my heart. I have locked them away, well hidden from the world. And while I don't think everything about everyone should be shared, I think I have held back parts of me that perhaps I should have freely given.

It is scary to share the innermost parts of one's soul, one's beliefs. There's a chance they might be ridiculed or taken lightly. Such sharing leaves me feeling exposed, vulnerable for all to see and all to judge. I like protection. I like safety.

In writing this book, I feel that I have taken all of my hidden feelings and laid them out in the light. I wanted to share this—the embarrassing, the uncomfortable, the hideously disfigured emotions right along with the beautiful, the sacred, the overwhelmingly divine—because when Russell died, I wanted someone to share it with me. I didn't want clichés. I didn't want to hear that time would make it better. I didn't want to hear how someone survived it well, to hear the joy they now had because of it.

I wanted the pain. I wanted the gore. I wanted the horrible ugliness that consumed me for a time. I wanted validation for my roller coaster of emotions.

I read many books. Some filled the need to connect emotionally with another grieving mother, but most did not. Most were written years after the child had died, and while factual, they lacked raw emotion. The authors were not sensitive, tender, skinned alive, and bleeding without mercy or respite.

First I had to write Russell's biography. Then I was able to start this book. I was compelled to write my memories and my experiences to *keep* them grotesque and monstrous—in short, to tell the truth about my grief.

And now that it is done, I am satisfied.

But I am like my old missionary companion. I'm afraid to share it. Afraid that others may see it and judge it and judge me because of it. Now that I see it in the light of day, I see how ugly it was. I'm tempted to pull it in, to hide it deep in the recesses of my memory, to lock it up and throw away the key.

I'm not comfortable exposing my inadequacies and my shortcomings. I suppose few people are. I have never felt more vulnerable, less in control, or lower in my life than I have since Russell died. Yet I've never felt more loved, more important, and more sure of the power my Savior has to make everything all right.

# Acknowledgments

THE BEST PART ABOUT WRITING this book is remembering how friends, neighbors, and family reached out to my grieving family. Writing an acknowledgments page is scary business for me; there are simply too many people to thank, too many people who loved my family in our time of need. I am eternally indebted to all for your thoughtful gestures, your kind words, and your sweet acts of service to us. I am blessed to know you, and my life is better because you are in it.

Melanie and Rachel, thank you for reading my story and helping me get it to this point. You gave me great insights and were fabulous guides in the world of writing and publishing. Annette, I'm still touched at your generosity in editing a book you knew nothing about. I have no idea how many hours you gave to me, but it was a beautiful gift that I'm grateful for.

Geralene and Randy, you have always been great examples to us. When it was time to let friends know the sad news, you were the first ones we called. You mobilized our rescue and continue to be amazing friends.

Alison and John, I don't even have words for you. I only know a portion of what you did for us, but I know you quietly did so much more behind the scenes. You both mean so much to me, and I'm grateful for our friendship. Alison, you were the first to read this book and encourage me to do something with it. Thank you.

Nikki, you never forgot me, and that means more than you'll ever know.

Sheridan, thank you for your friendship and our brother swaps.

Jenn, you are never afraid to make me cry by talking about Russell. I love to hear his name, even if it makes me emotional. I also love my Cailyn hugs.

Bethany, everyone should have a go-to person. Thanks for being mine.

Tania, you are the most selfless giver I know. I think we were friends in heaven. And by the way, thanks for the teddy bears.

Brittany, I treasure the scrapbooks you helped make, and I treasure our friendship.

Karen Gerdts, you had just suffered a loss yourself, and yet you were there for my family and me in so many significant ways. You are a quietly profound teacher.

Carrie Clark, although we mourn different losses, thank you for being a grieving partner.

Elaine, I have learned much from your example of finding the blessings in each trial.

Bonnie, thank you for being a friend, a listening ear, a shoulder to cry on, a therapist, an example. Your visits helped me move forward and get through that first year.

Karina and Kami, if I were given the chance to pick more sisters, I'd pick you. Karen, you've always been an example and a friend. I look to you for comfort and guidance. Thank you for raising such a great son.

Heather and Darwin, I'm glad this sad experience has brought us so much closer. Thank you for checking up on me. Betsey and Eric, the thought of our loved ones hanging out in heaven together makes me smile. Randy, thank you for letting me rant when I needed to. Brett and Amy, in those first awful months, you called every few weeks. I will never be able to explain adequately how important those phone calls were to me. Liza and Steven, Brian and Liz, and Rex, I wish we lived closer to each other. It would be fun to hang out with you guys.

Mom and Dad, my testimony of Jesus Christ is the only thing that got me through this experience. Thank you for being true to your beliefs through the years and being the examples you are. I am grateful that you gave me experiences as a child that helped foster my testimony and a deep love for the scriptures.

Karissa, thank you for all of your hugs and for remembering Russell in your prayers.

Kyle, thank you for wanting me to be normal—it gave me a goal to shoot for.

Jake, thank you for making me smile. And no, you can't have a cut of the royalties just because your name is in this book.

Joey, thank you for not growing up too fast.

Russell, thank you for the memories and for giving us something to look forward to. My only request is for you to be more conspicuous when you visit.

Kirk, I love you more than words can say. You are my husband, my love, and my life. Life with you is an amazing adventure. With your organization and my tenacity, we have become a phenomenal team, and I am forever grateful to be sealed to you so that our adventure can continue on eternally.

I don't really love this new road I'm on, but I love where it is leading me. And I love my traveling companions.

# Chapter One
## THAT FATEFUL DAY

I AM A BEREAVED MOTHER.

*Bereaved* describes my emotional status, but it doesn't explain for whom I am bereaved. It doesn't tell you that I suddenly and unexpectedly lost my little boy in an accident on the last day of our Christmas vacation. Our vibrant, happy, energetic little boy was there one minute, and then, in one horrifying day and without warning, he was gone.

If my parents died, I could say I was an orphan. If my husband died, I would be a widow. As it is, there is no word, no title to bear the burden of my grief. When someone asks, "How many children do you have?" and the follow-up, "What are their ages?" I get a pit in my stomach, my heart races, my breathing becomes shallow, and I panic as I decide how much information to give.

I am a bereaved mother, and there is no good way to explain it.

\* \* \*

January 1, 2008—a day associated with new beginnings and resolutions—was the day that life as I knew it was shattered. On this day, the last day of our vacation to Provo, Utah, I was pushed across the line of normalcy and fell into an abyss.

This was to be our last full day of our fun vacation because the next day we were leaving for home. We were an active family, one that loved the outdoors. We camped, hiked, rock climbed, mountain biked, kayaked, and explored. Even with a baby in tow—and for quite a number of years, we always seemed to have a baby in tow—we enjoyed playing in nature.

We were just a normal family, insanely busy with five young children to entertain. Karissa was eleven, Kyle was nine, Jake was seven, Russell was impatiently waiting for his fifth birthday only a few weeks away, and Joey was twenty-one months old. My husband, Kirk, had been called as bishop the year before, and we finally felt like we were "hitting the groove." Trips were easier now that everyone was a bit older, and I was getting used to Kirk's busy schedule. If I had been asked about my life that New Year's Eve, I would have said it had never been better.

This was our first family trip to Utah. We left the day after Christmas 2007. Kirk's sister Karina and her family had recently moved from California to Provo, and since we had lived so close to each other in California, we had often been together. It was hard to see them move so far away, especially just before Christmas.

To lessen the blow, we decided to spend the rest of our vacation with them. It was a big Hess family caravan, consisting of our family, Kirk's other sisters and their families, and Grandma Hess, Kirk's mom. Our children were excited to see their cousins again and couldn't wait to experience Utah with them. Karissa looked forward to playing in the snow nonstop, and the boys couldn't wait for the fun of scheming with their cousins. Kirk anticipated all of the family memories we'd create.

And yet, while everyone else was excited for the trip, I wasn't. I wanted to see Karina and her family, but the thought of packing the car and driving such a distance with all of the children wasn't appealing. I didn't want to go. I didn't have any premonitions or *bad* feelings about the trip; I just felt a heaviness about it that I couldn't shake. I kept hoping it would be cancelled or that Kirk would decide it was too much and we would just stay home. I kept thinking of when I was a child and my family took yearly summer trips to Utah. It was an excruciatingly hot, boring, and *long* ride. I chalked my unease up to those painful memories and packed a number of car activities.

Unbeknownst to me, other people had had intuitive feelings about the outcome of our trip. A family friend was on his way into a store when he was struck by a feeling so powerful and intense that he actually stopped walking. He felt like someone in our family was going to die on the trip, and he was filled with sadness and sympathy, as if he'd just heard the news. It was such a random but forceful experience that he told his wife about it when he got home. They debated telling us and finally decided against it because it seemed so implausible. I'm glad they didn't say anything. It wouldn't have changed the outcome, but it might have made us feel like we *could* have changed things somehow.

Another friend had a compulsive feeling to see me and give me a hug before we left. We were both really busy with the Christmas holiday and struggled to connect. My friend felt funny showing up at my house just to give me a hug but felt like she needed to. She couldn't understand why; she just felt like I would be going away for a long, long time to a discouraging, dark place. She felt she had to come by to give me comfort before we left. Because it all sounded so weird to her, she didn't mention her unease until later. Instead, she made a plate of cookies—she *never* baked cookies—as an excuse to drop by.

Our four-year-old son, Russell, on the other hand, was totally excited. He missed his cousin Isaac and couldn't wait for all the fun they'd have together. As I agonized about what to pack and what food to bring, Russell decided to help. He took a handful of brown paper lunch bags and filled them with canned foods and goodies from our pantry. He lined them up in our garage and proudly showed me. I remember smiling at his innocence as I rifled through those bags and saw canned fruits and vegetables along with cans of soup and condensed milk—plus a bag of marshmallows and some fruit snacks.

When we got to Utah, Karina's husband, David, had set up an amazing itinerary for us—we all stayed at his brother John's house so we could take advantage of every minute together. With nine adults and twelve kids, we were a noisy and busy bunch. We swam in their indoor/outdoor pool. We visited his brother's cabin in the canyon. We saw the lights at Temple Square. We visited my grandma and an aunt and an uncle. The adults enjoyed the cozy warmth inside while all of the cousins played together in the snow. We braved the freezing cold and went sledding again and again and again. The children enjoyed the snow, but Russell, who was an extremely cautious kid, found that he *loved* sledding and proclaimed himself the "sledding master." Every day flew by in a whirlwind of joy, and then we had one last day to fill before it was time to go home: January 1, 2008.

The day started out normally, some children waking up at the crack of dawn, others trying to sleep in as long as possible. We could all feel the fun of the trip winding down, and we were a little grumpy with each other that morning. All I could see were the mountains of laundry I'd have to do when we returned home. I imagined the hours it would take to load up the car for our painfully long and drawn-out drive back.

We spent the morning debating how best to fill the day. Some wanted to go to a dinosaur museum, some wanted to go sledding again, and others wanted to take it easy. We decided to do a little sightseeing, go to lunch, and then finish the afternoon with sledding at Rock Canyon Park. A group of us loaded into the car, and we drove up Provo Canyon. We watched some crazy guys ice climbing up Bridal Veil Falls, then we drove to the Missionary Training Center.

On the way over, we were listening to U2's song, "Sometimes You Can't Make It on Your Own."

Russell piped up. "Dad, I don't think we should listen to this song anymore." When asked why we should turn it off, Russell said, "Because the guy keeps singing, 'Sometimes you get naked on your own,' and that's not very nice."

We kept trying to explain the real lyrics, but he kept insisting that we were the ones getting it wrong. In the end, we just turned off the song, admonishing him to *not* tell the cousins we were listening to songs about getting naked.

Grandma Hess stayed in the car with our youngest, Joey, who'd fallen asleep, and the rest of us walked into the MTC. We expected a wild group like us to be kicked out at any time. Instead, everyone smiled and let us stay. We went to the big map and told the children to point to where they wanted to go on their missions. Jake chose Egypt, Karissa chose anywhere in Europe, and Kyle chose China.

"I don't know where I want to go," Russell said with a shrug.

We snapped pictures of the children pointing to their picks on the map, and we told Russell to just point anywhere. He pointed up.

We didn't know that the moment was prophetic. Russell was pointing heavenward, and he'd be starting his mission in heaven later that day.

We walked out to the MTC sign and took pictures of each child by it. We made Russell take a serious picture then let him be silly in the group shot. Usually we aren't that picky about our children taking serious pictures—most of the pictures we have of our children are with silly expressions—but somehow, this time in front of the Missionary Training Center sign, I felt like Russell needed to have a regular smile on his face. He wasn't very happy about it, and we ended up taking more pictures than we wanted just to get a normal-looking one. That picture now hangs in our living room, along with the one of Russell pointing heavenward, and the words:

I hope they call me on a mission
When I have grown a foot or two.
I hope by then I will be ready
To teach and preach and work as missionaries do.

MISSION CALL: JANUARY 1, 2008

RUSSELL IS NOW SERVING IN THE
PARADISE SOUTH MISSION.

(Kirk chose the word *south* because he figured most of the missionary work would be done at the south end of paradise, where he assumes the spirit prison is.)

As we watched the missionaries walking from the temple, we talked about how great missions were and how much the children were going to enjoy theirs.

When we finished, we went back to Karina's home. Russell didn't want to put his boots on just to go inside from the car, so I carried him across the street. As I put him down, I felt something suspicious in his pocket and discovered a handful of Legos he had swiped from Isaac's stash. I talked to him about stealing, and I could tell he felt guilty. We returned the Legos, and Russell seemed to feel much better.

Looking back, although I know little children who die before the age of accountability are taken straight into the arms of the Father, I'm often tempted to wonder if Russell would have stayed on earth a little longer if I hadn't made him return the Legos. Would his spirit have been as pure and ready to enter heaven if he had stolen Legos in his pocket?

I went downstairs to measure a window that Karina wanted a curtain for, and the children all ran downstairs to play with toys. Karina and Grandma Hess later told me that when the other children were running downstairs to play, Russell went to the living room. Karina was there, changing her son's diaper. Russell sat on one of the big overstuffed chairs and looked out the window. Karina thought it was strange for Russell to be sitting alone instead of following the others to the toys, so she told him he could go downstairs and play.

"I know," he said. "I just want to sit here for a minute."

Karina left him there, lost in his four-year-old thoughts while looking at the snow-covered mountains.

It was so out of place for Russell to just sit staring out a window that Grandma Hess noticed too. Neither Grandma nor Karina thought much of it until later. Now we wonder how much Russell knew then about his upcoming mission. I wonder if he saw deceased family in the window. His grandpa and great-grandpa had passed on many years before. I imagine them waving, smiling, and saying something like, "See you soon!"

When we finished our activities at the house, we went to lunch and said good-bye to those who were going on to Salt Lake for a few more days, and then the rest of us went to Rock Canyon Park.

The park sat just behind the Provo Temple and in front of Rock Canyon. It had a playground on a hill and, below, a huge grassy area then covered with snow. The grassy area was bowl shaped, with ridges on all sides. It seemed to be the perfect sledding park with launching points everywhere along the bowl. The area by the playground was the tallest part of the hill. That was where we parked the car and began. The bottom ridge of the park had sledding on either side of its bowl shape. We didn't realize it at the time, but school was starting the next day for the locals, so it was their last day for sledding. It seemed like there were thousands of people sledding inside and outside of the bowl, testing their mettle on the longer ride from the top or on the shorter one closer to the bottom of the park.

It was utter and complete mayhem with so many children and families. People were accidentally crashing into each other and running over others. We saw many near misses and painful collisions. The adults in our group commented on how dangerous sledding seemed to be. We watched in horror as sledder after sledder narrowly missed crashing into a wood post in the middle of the bowl. I had lived in Massachusetts until I was eight and remembered getting slammed a few times while sledding, but I hadn't been sledding since. Obviously, the dangers were still around. The children didn't seem too worried though.

Russell was in his element. He grabbed a sled and took off with an enthusiastic, "Woo hoo!" Jake was a little more cautious, finding a more mellow slope. Kyle and Karissa were animals, looking for the fastest and steepest rides—until Kyle crashed at the bottom and decided he didn't like sledding anymore. I held Joey as I kept watch on everyone.

Russell and Kirk would be easy to keep track of, Russell in a red one-piece snowsuit and huge smile, and Kirk in his red puffy snow jacket. Kirk and I took pictures and videos, then he and Russell were off and running. I took Joey down a few times before I took Jake to the bathroom because he wasn't feeling well and before Kyle found me and told me he was still hurting from his fall and wanted to go home.

I was trying to console Kyle, watch Jake—who was resting on a bench by the bathroom—and keep a wiggly Joey from slipping down the hill. At about that moment, I realized I couldn't see Russell or Kirk. I assumed they were together, but I didn't know where. I wasn't panicked, but I felt like I *needed* to find them. It was an insistent, compelling feeling forceful enough to keep me looking for them as I wrestled with Joey. As I walked back and forth across the top of the bowl, scanning for a red suit and puffy jacket, I kept spotting a little blonde girl in a red suit instead. My eyes darted over the expanse of sledders and kept being drawn back to that girl and her darned red snowsuit. I walked to the steep section and found Karissa and her cousin. By that time, Kyle felt better and had joined them. I half carried, half dragged Joey to the other side, where I found more members of our family. By this time I was starting to feel a bit panicked. I still couldn't see Kirk or Russell.

I remember thinking, *What if Russell has been kidnapped?* and suddenly a strong, warm feeling enveloped me, almost melting me inside from my head to my toes. The thought came to me that Russell was sealed to me and that he was mine *no matter what.* The sensation came on so suddenly and strongly that I stopped walking. Then, as quickly as it had come, it was gone and replaced with a renewed urgency to find Kirk and Russell.

I was puzzled by the sudden and overwhelming warmth and comfort of Russell being sealed to me. At the time, I didn't analyze it. It was significant, I knew, but my concentration on finding him and Kirk was so intense that I couldn't focus on anything else.

When I came upon Karina and Grandma Hess and expressed my concern, they weren't worried at all, which left me feeling disgruntled. In fact, they were getting ready to leave for Karina's house to get food for her baby.

Even when I emphasized how worried I was, they still went home, leaving me behind and feeling angry. Here I was, holding a crazed toddler and freaking out because of the urgency inside me, and they were just driving away. I realized I hadn't asked them for help, but I couldn't believe they hadn't even offered.

I was still fuming when minutes later their car returned. They lowered a window and Karina yelled, "Russell has been in an accident! He's going to the hospital in an ambulance!"

Feeling little more than disbelief, I flew into action. I didn't take the time to sort out Karina's words. My body seemed to take over as I collected Jake from the bathroom, with Joey still wiggling in my arms. I handed him over to Grandma, then I ran to get the big children while Karina and Grandma started throwing the little ones into the car.

My heart was pounding, my brain turning in circles. I couldn't process what I had just heard. Russell in an *accident?* Bad enough for an *ambulance?* Even with all of the crashes I had seen that day, I couldn't fathom how badly Russell must have crashed to be rushed to the hospital.

"It must be a broken leg or something," I whispered not so confidently to myself. I wouldn't allow myself to think any deeper on the subject. Instead,

I turned off my brain and let my body stay in charge as I ran with the older children to the car.

I later learned that Kirk and Russell had started out sledding at the far end of the bottom of the bowl. An adventurous Russell had asked Kirk to explore new runs with him. They had gone down inside the bowl a few times, and then Russell had wanted to go down on the outside.

They'd gone over the hill to survey the run. It wasn't very steep. There was a group of trees to the left and the street to the right, but each was far enough over that they felt they didn't need to worry. Russell really wanted to go down, so Kirk chose the safest place to start. He had no uneasy feelings, no apprehension or warning whatsoever, so off they went. On their way down, the tube turned, hit a dip in the hill, and sent them racing backward toward the trees. Kirk knew they were moving fast. Instinctively, he covered Russell in a big bear hug so Kirk would take the brunt of the impact.

Russell, sensing no danger, yelled in Kirk's ear, "This is the *best* day ever!"

That's when they hit the tree. On impact, Kirk sustained bruising and a few broken ribs. But when they came to a stop, Russell wasn't moving. Kirk gently laid him down. Somehow, Russell's head had hit the tree. He was breathing, but he had blood running out of his ears, and though his teeth were locked shut, Kirk knew Russell's mouth was also filled with blood.

A few people who had witnessed the accident came to help. Kirk threw them his phone so they could call 911. And then someone on the scene administered a blessing while Kirk stabilized Russell's neck and head. The ambulance arrived within minutes.

Then Kirk had a terrible choice to make: should he ride to the hospital with his unconscious, seriously wounded son, or should he find me to tell me what had happened? He had the car keys and worried we'd be stranded if he left. So Kirk left Russell in the paramedics' care and raced up the hill.

It was at that critical moment that Karina and Grandma were driving through the intersection that would have taken them out of the parking lot. Miraculously, they happened to glance in the opposite direction as they were turning and saw the ambulance heading into the park at the bottom of the hill.

If they had been a minute or two later or earlier, they would have missed everything. As it was, they noticed the ambulance and were turning their attention back to the front of the car when they both saw Kirk running full tilt at the top of the hill. He was still a ways away, but they recognized his red jacket. Screeching the car to a stop, they both got out and began to run toward him.

They reached Kirk, got his keys and the little information he had, and raced back to get me, allowing Kirk to make it in time to go with Russell.

While he had been sitting in the snow with Russell, Kirk felt his dad's presence. His dad had died twenty-nine years before, when Kirk was a child, but Kirk didn't stop to wonder if he was there to give comfort and support or to take Russell to heaven; he just knew at this desperate time that when he needed his father's strength the most, his dad was there.

We had a lot of heavenly intervention that day. Looking back, we were able to see the Lord's hand gently guiding us through what would surely be the most difficult day of our lives.

The ambulance drove cautiously until it was about halfway to the hospital. Then someone told the driver to get there ASAP—Russell had stopped breathing, and his heart had stopped beating.

Meanwhile, back at the park, we were throwing children in the car. My brother-in-law David gave me a ride to the hospital, while Karina and Grandma Hess drove the kids to David's brother's home. I was sick with worry but also felt that all would be okay. I kept thinking of a teenage boy in our ward who'd been in a car accident a few weeks before and had ended up in a coma. Our ward had held a special fast for him, and he and his family had been in all of our family prayers. The boy miraculously came out of the coma the day after the fast. I knew the power of the priesthood was real; I'd experienced that power and seen its influence many times in my life.

As we drove to the hospital, I held on to the comfort that Kirk held the priesthood. It became my mantra while I pled for the safety of my little boy. I wasn't allowing myself to think that Russell was in real trouble; I was worried that maybe he needed surgery or that he broke an arm or leg. I had no idea how serious the situation really was, but I continued to feel that all would be well. And yet I was shaking uncontrollably. I couldn't understand it—I wasn't calm, but I felt that everything would be okay.

I sat there reminding God that Kirk had the priesthood and asking Him to please be mindful of my little boy when all of a sudden I thought of Kirk and how awful I would have felt if it had been *me* there, seeing our little Russell hurt. I felt impressed not to say anything negative to Kirk when I saw him—even if we were dealing with only a broken leg. I instantly knew I couldn't joke around or say anything that would make Kirk feel bad or responsible. He would already be feeling terrible and vulnerable, and I was told I needed to give him extra comfort, hold his hand, and put my arm around him. I felt empathetic toward him and the feelings he must be having, and I felt a great love for him. I trusted him completely and knew he was not at fault. I wasn't angry with him because I knew an accident could have happened just as easily with me and Russell on the sled.

As we rode to the hospital, I knew I was not alone in the car that day. I had specific thoughts and directions come to my mind that I know were not mine. It was as if a woman were sitting next to me with her arm around me, instructing me on how to act and what to do when I saw Kirk at the hospital.

I still wonder who this guardian angel was. One day I will find out and thank her for giving me specific instructions for the horrible situation that followed.

We got to the ambulance entrance at the emergency room, and I debated for a moment if I was allowed to go through the door. Would I get in trouble? How would I find Kirk? How would I find Russell? Should I go through the regular entrance? I didn't even know where it was. As if in answer to prayer, Kirk and two men rounded the corner and pulled me inside. Everything seemed to be happening on fast-forward. It appeared there was little time left.

But left for *what*?

I was unable and unwilling to think more on this question as they escorted me into a little room down the hall.

The first man, Fred, seemed to be in charge. He introduced the other man as Dr. Swanson, Russell's emergency room doctor. My head was already spinning, and my heart throbbed in my throat as we sat poised on the edge of our seats, staring nervously at each other. So much stress and energy filled the room that I felt like bolting out the door.

Dr. Swanson began. "Russell's heart isn't beating, and he isn't breathing on his own." He described the different procedures they had done to determine why and to revive him, but Russell wasn't responding to anything. I waited for him to tell me what they would do next to fix Russell, but he didn't. In his silence, I realized he had nothing more to say.

"What will you do if Russell's heart starts beating and he starts breathing on his own?" I asked.

"Then we'll airlift him to Primary Children's." Dr. Swanson's tone implied that this was unlikely.

I sat in shock. Surely I was in the wrong room talking to the wrong doctor.

It all seemed surreal. How could *this* be real? I felt as if I had wandered into some alternate reality—one in which I obviously did not belong. My brain fought against accepting the doctor's words. It was all so far-fetched, like being caught up in someone else's life—a fictional story on television maybe. Yet there I was. My mind could not deny the truth no matter how hard it tried.

The exchange with Dr. Swanson probably lasted only a few seconds, minutes at the most. Yet, looking back, it seemed to have lasted much longer. The memory feels jumbled, as if it was so caustic, so damaging that it destroyed my ability to recall it normally. I can see the little square grieving room, with its uncomfortable chairs and squat couches. I can see a phone on an end table in the corner. But try as I might, I can't recall Dr. Swanson's or Fred's face. I *think* Dr. Swanson was tall and Fred had dark hair, but I don't know for sure. When I revisit the memory, I don't see much. I just feel those horrific emotions at hearing the appalling news that my son was dying.

Dr. Swanson asked if we would like to see Russell. Fred warned us that there were more people in the room than usual. But even with the warning, I wasn't prepared for the scene. How in the world could anyone be prepared for something like that? The ambulance workers who brought Russell in had stayed to see what they could do. Surgeons and doctors from the hospital had come down to volunteer their assistance. And nurses and assistants had poured in from all around to give whatever help they could.

"When a child is in trouble," Fred explained, "everyone wants to help."

He kept talking, explaining things the entire time. His voice seemed to drone on; I couldn't focus enough to comprehend many of his words. At times I thought, *Why is he still talking? There's too much noise and confusion for him to be talking.* At other times his words were comforting.

Strangely, the comments I did hear and comprehend are now precious to me. Fred was our guide through this, and he wanted to make sure he was giving us all the information he could to help us navigate the horror before us and what would come later as we tried to make sense of it.

Even as Dr. Swanson prepared us for the worst, I kept feeling that Heavenly Father could fix this. After all, Kirk had the priesthood, and through that priesthood, miracles were not only possible but could not be withheld. I had absolute faith that Russell could be healed. I knew the power of God was strong enough to fix even this. I had a knowledge that it *could* happen.

I didn't have time to ponder if it *would*.

The sight of my little boy lying naked and lifeless on the table stopped me short. Seeing Russell like this—unresponsive, his open eyes not seeing, his limbs limp, the unnatural color of his skin—told me his spirit was already gone. To where, I did not know. I remember looking up at the ceiling to see if I could see his spirit, but he was nowhere to be seen or even felt.

Did that mean Russell was already dead? He couldn't be dead, not yet. Not my little boy! The doctors were still rushing around, doing everything in their power to bring him back. But if they had to bring him *back*. . . . It was too overwhelming a thought, and I pushed it out of my mind. There were doctors all over him, making his heart beat, making him breathe. His body couldn't really be dead if his heart was beating and his lungs were filling with air, could it?

I didn't have an answer. I just knew that while I saw my sweet little son lying on the table, something about him was missing. And while I couldn't feel or see his spirit, I knew it had to be close. I knew Russell could see me, I knew he was leaving, but I also knew he could still come back to me.

Fred said we could get close to Russell. He said again and again how rare it was for us to have permission to touch Russell at this point in the emergency. As the doctors and nurses made room for us, I could still hear Fred talking—*why was he still talking?*—about what an exceptional opportunity it was for us to be this close. We stroked Russell's cheek, his hair. I know I whispered things like, "Russell, please come back. We need you." I sensed that he could hear me. I told him I wanted him to stay, but in my heart I was beginning to realize he was gone and wasn't coming back.

Even at this point, my faith didn't waver. I knew all Russell needed was "to touch the hem of Jesus' cloak" and the color and life would return to his body. I knew that though it looked bleak, he *could* be made whole and new again. There was no doubt there. I was given a transcendent, powerful witness that, yes, my Savior *could* fix this. He *could* heal Russell. I had the faith sufficient for it to happen. The Lord was close, close enough to touch. The veil was thin. I could not feel the presence of my son, but I felt the all-encompassing presence of my Elder Brother. The Savior was more real to me at that moment than He had ever been before.

As I looked into Russell's unfocused eyes, I felt Heavenly Father's love for Russell coursing through my body. I felt His love and concern for *me*, His daughter. I felt His concern and His sorrow too. As we were gently ushered away from Russell, I felt my Savior's presence even more keenly. My belief in His healing power was stronger than ever. I *knew* Russell could be healed. I *knew* he could jump off the table into my arms at the Lord's command. It was not faith. It was not hope. It was a total knowledge of the power of my Savior. It was an awesome moment to be engulfed in the knowledge of the miracles that are possible through the power of God.

But, as I looked at my lifeless little boy, the realization came to me by degrees that this was not to be *my* miracle. Surprisingly, this was not a bitter moment. My faith in Christ's *power* was surpassed by my faith in *Him* and in my Heavenly Father's plan. And while I had the faith for my little boy to be healed, I also had the faith to let him go if that was my Father's will. I was desperately sad but not desperate. I was not despondent. I was not wretched.

I didn't consciously think these things at the time, but I felt them. The Lord was next to me, and I felt close to Him. I felt acceptance in my heart, even though I knew losing my boy would break it. As I stood there holding Kirk's hand and looking upon the chaos in the room, I felt I was in a sacred place. I was no longer in a cramped emergency room in Utah. We had all been lifted halfway to heaven, and Christ, with a legion of angels, had come halfway down to meet us. I could feel His and their love flow through my very being.

This transcendent experience was only seconds long. All of these feelings and thoughts had rushed through me as the doctors again flooded in and tried to revive Russell. It may sound like I was prepared and ready for the worst. But I wasn't. The stark reality of the moment ripped me from my momentary reprieve.

As Kirk and I moved out of the way, the efforts to bring my son back seemed violent and loud. They pumped Russell's chest, squeezing air into a tube down his throat. People were everywhere, bustling around, moving faster than I could think. It was busy and overwhelming and chaotic.

I know it was organized chaos, but it all moved so fast. I kept wanting to say, "Wait, wait, wait," but it didn't stop or slow down. In all of this, I felt not peace—who could feel peace at a moment like this?—but I felt comfort. I felt calm. I felt assured. I had been able to be close to Russell, to hold his hand, to touch his face.

But now Kirk and I clutched each other in shock and denial. All I could do was whisper, "Oh, Russell, please come back."

Dr. Swanson came over and gently asked us the worst thing imaginable: "We are ready to call it. Is that okay?"

I'd just gotten there, and they were done. It was too fast. It was too soon, too much. While it was apparent he couldn't stay, I couldn't believe Russell would ever really die.

Not yet!

I told Dr. Swanson they couldn't call it. "Are you sure *everything* has been done?"

Dr. Swanson assured me it had. A woman asked how long Russell had been down. They determined it had been ten minutes on the way to the hospital then about another twenty there. They had been performing CPR for twenty-five to thirty minutes.

"Can I call it?" Dr. Swanson quietly asked again.

*It is his time.* This time I heard it in my head and felt it in my heart.

Later, when I was at home, I realized the hospital staff had performed CPR far longer than they needed to. They probably knew after five minutes—maybe even right away—that Russell would not be coming back. They had kept Russell's body alive so that I could say good-bye. So that Kirk and I could have one last moment and one last memory with Russell before he moved on. I will be eternally grateful for their gift.

In that moment in the ER, I felt the Lord nearby again, His arms around me, gently whispering comfort to my heart. This *was* Russell's time. I didn't even think to question it. This was the way it had to be; the fact was unmistakable. This was part of the Lord's plan for Russell and for us. This was not a tragic accident that could have been avoided; it was part of a beautiful master plan extending into the eternities. I found in my heart that I could let Russell go into the arms of his Heavenly Father.

With all my heart I wanted Russell to stay. But I would accept the answer I was being given. I would trust in my Heavenly Father.

It occurred to me that I was having a "but if not" moment, like the three courageous Israelites of old, Shadrach, Meshach, and Abednego, who, for refusing to break their covenants with the Lord, were threatened with a fiery death by King Nebuchadnezzar. Trusting in the Lord, they answered the king: "If it be so, our God whom we serve is able to deliver us from the burning fiery furnace, and he will deliver us out of thine hand, O king. *But if not*, be it known unto thee O king, that we will not serve thy gods, nor worship the golden image which thou hast set up."[1]

Kirk asked only to give Russell a father's blessing before they stopped CPR. What happened next would have been funny if it hadn't been so sad, but about six or seven people shouted out, "I've got oil!" and "I can anoint!" We were definitely in Utah, where a father's last blessing is not only understood but encouraged and revered.

In this beautiful blessing, Kirk asked Russell to come back but also gave him permission to go, assuring him of our great love for him and our hope that he would enjoy fulfilling his mission on the other side of the veil.

When he finished, we stepped back, arm in arm, and watched as Dr. Swanson looked up at the clock and announced the time of death. The intensity of the room gradually calmed down into a reverent quiet as the doctors stopped trying to revive Russell. One by one they stepped away from our little boy and allowed us to stand by his side one more time. The only noise in the room now was the gut-wrenching flatline of the heart monitor. Someone mercifully clicked it off.

As the nurses stepped in to unhook him from all the machines and then wrapped his little body in a cozy blanket, I still felt, even then, that Russell could come back. But I knew he wouldn't. Although the miracle of Jairus's daughter[2] would not be my miracle, in that sacred place as I stroked my precious child's cheek, I felt the fullness of the Father's plan.

And *that* was my miracle. That there was a plan and this was part of it.

Of course I would have preferred Russell to jump from the table into my embrace, but as they placed my dead son's lifeless body into my arms, I realized I'd be okay. Heavenly Father had not forsaken my family. He'd had ample time and opportunity to bring Russell back. The fact that He hadn't done so was another testimony to me that it was time for Russell to go home. And for now, that was enough.

We sat there, Kirk and I, in the now-still emergency room, with little Russell in our arms. One orderly silently cleaned the room around us, trying to circumvent our grief. We cried. We sobbed. We hugged. We cried again. They were not bitter tears, but they were full of sorrow. Our hearts had gone to heaven with Russell and felt as if they were being ripped out of our chests.

Kirk kept saying, "I'm sorry, I'm sorry." He felt totally responsible.

I told him I didn't feel he was. I'm grateful Heavenly Father let me know it was Russell's time. I honestly felt that if it hadn't happened while sledding, it would have happened in another way.

It had to happen—I knew it. It was Russell's time to go back to heaven. And I'm thankful Kirk was with our son when he died. Russell didn't die alone, afraid, or even hurt. He was having the best day of his life, doing the thing he loved most, his dad holding him tight. One minute Russell was in his dad's arms, the next he was encircled about in the arms of his Savior and grandpa and great-grandpa. What a beautiful experience that must have been for him!

And while Kirk struggled with feelings of guilt, he was strengthened by the certainty that his dad had been there to take Russell across the veil. As we'd held Russell at the hospital, Kirk had felt our son go from our arms into his dad's.

I'm grateful Kirk's dad was there, and I wonder if he had any say in when Russell was to go home. I'm sure Grandpa Kyle was excited to see Kirk—and knew the veil would be thin when he collected Russell. I imagine Grandpa Kyle was also apprehensive about how this experience would hurt his son and probably tried to exude as much love, acceptance, peace, comfort, and caring as possible so that one day Kirk could look back and feel it instead of the pain and confusion and desperation of the moment.

I like to picture Kirk in the snow, holding Russell, and Grandpa Kyle holding them both at the scene of the accident. And I'm grateful that Kirk was able to have that moment in the ER with his dad when Russell was called home. The more I ponder that day, the more I see the Lord's hand in it. While the emotions we experienced were excruciating and horrible, they were also tender and beautiful. It was a special, reverent, sacred time that would sustain us in the future.

When Kirk called Grandma Hess, David, and Karina to tell them the news, the children were all upstairs making get-well cards for Russell. No one expected what we had to say, of course. They all assumed he'd broken his leg like Isaac had the month before. Isaac kept saying that he would teach Russell how to use his wheelchair. We wanted to be the ones to tell our kids, so we asked that the adults not share the news with them before they were brought to the hospital.

When they arrived at the hospital, Karissa, Kyle, and Jake were asked to wait in the room where Kirk and I had first talked to the doctor. They still didn't know the full truth, but they started to worry when their cousins left them alone to take Joey for a walk around the hospital grounds.

Grandma Hess and Karina came into the room where we were still holding Russell. We cried and hugged and hugged and cried as we told them what happened. We recognized even then how the Lord had orchestrated the timing at Rock Canyon Park so Kirk could be in the ambulance and so I could get to the hospital. We saw the Lord's care and felt His love, and we were touched that He would give us so much in our time of need.

I knew I needed to go with Kirk to tell the kids, but I just couldn't leave Russell or put him back on the table. Grandma Hess offered to hold him for me. I shall be eternally grateful for her arms because placing my son in them was the only way I could leave him.

It was time to tell the kids. What could we say? How did one explain something so final, so painful, and so awful to their children? We had just experienced a closeness to the Savior that we'd never before felt, but that did not take away the pain or the great responsibility we now faced. How could we tell our children their brother had just died?

Kirk did most of the talking. I honestly don't remember much of what he said. I just remember being so proud to be married to such a strong, solid, amazing man. The children cried when they realized what their father was telling them. Kirk told about how he felt as a nine-year-old boy—our son Kyle's age—when he heard the news of his dad's death. He talked of temples, of forever, of how he'd sensed Grandpa Kyle there on the snowbank and in the ER with Russell. He talked about how we felt this was God's will and how it would be a sad thing to get used to but that Heavenly Father would help us. We sat there, clinging to each other, just sobbing. Jake's sobbing—loud and uncontrolled—broke my heart. He sounded like a wounded animal, as if he might break in two. Karissa and Kyle cried too but more quietly.

Karissa had a hard time understanding why Russell had died. She had said a quiet prayer at the house and felt a peace and a calm come over her. This was one of the few times she had felt the undeniable presence of the Holy Ghost. "But I felt that everything was going to be okay," she said in a voice full of confusion.

We told her that both Kirk and I had felt that same feeling before Russell died, and we both thought it had first meant that *he* would be okay. We explained that we hadn't realized that Heavenly Father was trying to tell us that *we* would be okay as well, just not the okay we expected. Heavenly Father was trying to give us comfort—something to fall back on—that this was His will and part of the plan.

There, in that quiet little room, our family made a pact that we *would* be okay. We would trust in God. We would help each other out. We wouldn't retreat and hide from this. We would become stronger. We would remember Russell and live righteously so we could be with him forever. We talked of the promise to children who die before they are accountable—that they are saved in the celestial kingdom (see D&C 137:10). Then we cried again. When we asked the children if they wanted to come say good-bye, they were ambivalent at first but then decided to. So we went together to the ER, where they said a short good-bye to Russell, who still lay encircled in his grandmother's arms. I lifted Russell out of Grandma's arms so I could hold him again, noting the stiffness that had set in while I'd been gone.

One by one, the other relatives quietly came in to say good-bye. Kirk's other sister's family had gone up to Salt Lake City but had come back as soon as they'd heard. After the children said their good-byes, Karina and David took all of them back to the house.

My parents in California were shocked, like the rest of us, when I told them the news. Being so far away made it harder for them to fathom the reality of it. They wanted to get on an airplane and join us at the hospital, but we saw the impossibility of it all. They called other family members. One of my aunts and two of my uncles living close by came to the hospital. It was comforting to have them there in our quiet little sanctuary. And it *was* a sanctuary. I felt very close to heaven. Although I felt the most overwhelming sorrow at the loss of my son, I felt that I could also see the big picture. I felt I could almost touch the eternities, and that helped ease my sorrow, even if just a little.

Nurses and attendants would come into the emergency room to clean up or get things. Out of the corner of my eye, I saw them walk in, stop, then shake their heads. Usually they clucked and muttered, "It's just not fair."

It almost made me laugh. No, life definitely wasn't fair. It's what I told my children when they wanted something other than what they got. No, life isn't fair, but isn't that why we are here? Life isn't fair, and that's part of the plan. How could I rant about life being unfair when I was trying to teach my children the very same lesson?

In those moments, my mind was opened and expanded to fully comprehend that mortal life *isn't* fair—and that's why it isn't forever. In that big sterile emergency room so far from home, I saw forever, and I resolved that while I may have to endure the indignities of an unfair existence, I would not be ranting and raving about it. I would not be bitter about the injustice of it all. I would be accepting of whatever my Heavenly Father required.

In my arms, Russell was starting to get heavy. How could his body be getting so heavy? How did death add weight to a body? Did the spirit make the body lighter? I was weary, but I was not ready to give him up yet. And Russell was getting so cold. He wasn't as cold as ice; he was more like the temperature of a marble statue in a cold room. His rosy cheeks were translucent white, as were his hands and the rest of his body. It was a color I had never seen before. What else is the color of death? I had never seen it this close up, and I morbidly marveled at the subtle changes that were transforming my little boy's body. It had become stiffened in the position I was holding him in. His lifeless hands were frozen in position now, open partway. I found myself rubbing his cold little hands as if I could massage the color, warmth, and life back into them.

It was at this point that Kirk gave me a blessing. *Where does he get the strength?* I wondered. The blessing was comforting until the end, when Kirk broke down and pleaded with me to forgive him for not protecting our son. After the blessing, I told him there was nothing to forgive—that this was part of the plan. I felt no anger, no animosity, no blame. Absolutely no blame. In fact, I felt gratitude that it was Kirk who'd been chosen for this burden. I couldn't have done it. I don't know how I would have survived thinking I was at fault. And it wasn't easy for Kirk. He struggled with the emotional pain for a long time. How my heart ached for him! I couldn't comprehend the guilt and pain he was feeling.

I'm grateful someone on the other side had come to prepare me in the car on the way to the hospital. How easy it would have been for me to lash out or say something thoughtless. Harsh words spoken at that time and place could never have been taken back. It scares me to think about how devastating and far-reaching our experience could have been had there been blame or anger present. It would have damaged our marriage in potentially irreparable ways. Had I not been open to the whisperings of the Spirit, I might have felt and said damaging things. *Grateful* is not adequate enough to express the thanks I feel to my Heavenly Father for giving me the information I needed to act correctly in this circumstance. This wasn't an easy moment for either of us by any means, but because we reached out to each other and trusted God, it became a sacred time.

Because I was able to see the plan and accept it, my love for my husband grew stronger as we sat in that cold hospital room. I didn't like what was happening, and I didn't want it, but I accepted it. And because of that, I was able to have an understanding that purged me of blame and anger and filled me with love.

When a man from the mortuary came to take Russell's body away, I panicked, realizing I would have to give him up. But no one rushed us. We took our time saying good-bye. I hugged Russell tight, not wanting to forget the freckles on his face, the way he felt, the memories that kept flooding back.

Finally, I felt I could let him go. We laid him on the table then hugged and cried some more. It was so hard to walk away. I had to go back a few more times just to touch his face, which, surprisingly, had grown even colder, even harder. One last hug, a kiss, an "I love you," and we left. In the corner of the room we found Russell's little red snowsuit torn open, crumpled, and discarded. The doctors had cut it off his little body in their efforts to save his life. Now it was ripped and bloody and broken, much like our new life.

A new life where everything had an unnatural quality to it. It was like we were in a different dimension. Things looked strangely familiar, and yet they were vastly different now in ways I couldn't put my finger on. It seemed like years since Russell had been alive. Had he really been laughing and talking to us only hours ago? It all seemed so far away, so distant and detached from this new life I was embarking on. And I felt really, really old. And drained.

As we walked out of the hospital, one of the ambulance workers clumsily tried to give us some comfort. "At least we know the plan of salvation," he said a little too heartily. I looked at him, my mind trying to process why he would be saying something like that to us in such a happy voice right now. It seemed so trite, so small when compared to the enormity of what had just happened.

He was smiling. *Why is he smiling?* My son was dead. My brows were furrowed as I continued to look at him questioningly. His smile faltered, and he stepped away.

I had just experienced a transcendent spiritual experience, but my heart was still broken. I could accept this event as part of Heavenly Father's plan, but simple phrases and "Sunday answers" felt empty and offensive and offered no comfort at all.

I don't even know what time it was when we pulled up to Karina's house. It felt late, years too late. It was dark outside, but it was winter, when the sun in Utah goes down obscenely early. We dragged ourselves in. Everything had changed. The mood of the house, the way everyone interacted with one another, the way they looked at us. We went downstairs, where the children were sleeping. Of course they were not sleeping.

Kirk and I cried again. The children had slept on mats on the floor during the trip, and Joey was next to them in a port-a-crib. They were all lying there in their spots. Russell's mat and sleeping bag looked lonely and forlorn in the middle. There was such an empty place on the floor without him. Surely he didn't really take up that much room?

But the empty space Russell left behind was much larger than that place on the ground. Kirk and I lay there, on the floor, in Russell's vacant spot, surrounded by our children. Even we couldn't fill the cavernous void.

Eventually Kirk and I lugged ourselves onto our bed. Every action seemed to take so much energy. Even falling asleep took more energy than I had. We lay there, each on our own side of the bed, not touching, not talking, both so lost in our own worlds that we were barely aware of the other. My mind kept seeing Russell naked and dead on the operating table. I had seen him alive today. Why couldn't I remember what he looked like then? I could only see him lifeless, unmoving. I could feel the weight and coolness of his body in my arms.

The night never seemed to end. Seconds stretched mercilessly into hours, barely ticking by. I remember looking at the clock on my night table again and again, perplexed that only minutes had passed when it felt like hours. I remember when the time finally said 12:03 and the date had changed from January 1 to January 2.

*Well, we made it to tomorrow*, I thought. It really did feel like an accomplishment. How in the world was I going to make it to next week? Next year?

## Chapter Two
## THE DAY AFTER

THE NEXT DAY WE WENT to the funeral home. They were kind and forgiving of our zombie-like states. First we had to pick out a casket. Weren't we too young to be doing this? We talked frankly and openly with the funeral home director. Since we would be buying a plot and planning the funeral in California, he gave us pointers and advice about all of the different things we would have to choose from once there. But we had to choose a casket now. And we had to choose how to carry Russell's body home. There, we would have to choose a plot and how we wanted Russell buried. Armed with information, I felt a bit more in control.

While making our selections, I was surprised at the things that now mattered to me. I'm a pretty frugal person by nature and always assumed I wouldn't go overboard if I had to bury someone. Not that I ever really thought much about it. But really, if the body was just going into the ground, what was the purpose of a fancy casket and all that? So I was surprised at my reaction when I saw the "line" of children's caskets. "Line," as in two. Both were hideously ugly, with some kind of blue or pink fur on the outside. And what was worse, these monstrosities cost an obscene amount. There was absolutely *no way* I would bury my boy in a furry blue casket. I didn't care what it cost—we'd spend our entire life savings to save Russell from such a fate. Even now I shudder at the thought of those repulsive caskets. Luckily, the man found us a nice "scratch and dent" (his words) wooden casket I could live with.

While leafing through a binder of old funeral programs, trying to get ideas for songs and musical numbers, I noticed that all of them were for *elderly* people. They had no funeral programs for children or even for young adults.

*Don't other people's children die occasionally?* I thought with a hint of bitterness. I set aside the binder, feeling utterly alone. So absolutely bereft and destitute.

On the way back from the funeral home, we stopped by Rock Canyon Park. We got out of the car and walked to the accident site. Since all the local children were back in school today, the park was eerily empty and quiet. Kirk pointed out the tree they had hit and recounted what had happened. We were like zombies walking around the tree, looking for a reason, *any* reason, to explain the drastic turn our lives had taken. But there was nothing. It looked like a regular hill covered in snow, with trees at the bottom. There were no chalk outlines, no flowers, nothing to signify the magnitude of events that had forever altered our lives less than twenty-four hours previous. In frustration, I stuck a stick in the snow next to the offending tree to mark the place in some small way. Then we slowly shuffled back to the car.

As we walked, Kirk posed a series of questions that changed the way I viewed Russell's death, the way I have tried to respond to it.

"What if, because of the way we were living before Russell died, one of our children wasn't going to make it to eternity with us? What if later in life, one of our children was going to start making choices contrary to God's plan? But what if Russell's death changed that? What if his death put us on a different road, causing us to parent differently and causing our children to choose differently? What if Russell's death was the catalyst to ensure that our *entire* family would live righteously enough to qualify for the sealing powers of the temple? Would that change the way you view the loss of Russell?"

Now, we'd done okay as parents. We had done all the "right" things, had done the best we could to raise our kids. But I knew that that was not enough to ensure they would turn out well. *Regardless* of our parenting, our children still had their agency and could use it any way they saw fit. They were just too young now to cause any real damage.

Hypothetically speaking, would I rather have Russell here for mortality if it meant losing one or more of our other children in immortality? What if Russell's death was the turning point that helped our children stay on the strait and narrow? What if they would now be making better choices *because* of Russell's death? Would I be okay with his death in that case, with such eternal implications?

Of course, there was only one possible answer. I could sacrifice my time on earth with my son if it meant my family could spend the eternities together.

Kirk then asked, "What if Russell's death wasn't to help anyone in our immediate family but was needed to change someone's life in our extended family? Would you let him go to save one of them?"

That question slowed me down a bit, but it still had the same answer. Of course I hated the thought of living the rest of my life without Russell, but what if it meant more of our family together in the eternities? The potential for good definitely outweighed the bad.

Then Kirk asked the hardest question of all. "What if Russell's death would not have made any changes to anyone's eternal outcome in our family but would help save the life of a complete stranger? Would you sacrifice your time on earth here with Russell now if learning about his story caused someone we don't even know to turn his life around and come closer to Christ?"

That question really made me think. What if I lost Russell not to save someone I loved and wanted to be in my eternal family unit but someone I didn't even know? What if hearing Russell's story would help someone I didn't necessarily even care about? Would I be as accepting of it then?

My answer would definitely have been different had Kirk asked me *before* Russell died. Would I have been willing to give up my son to save someone else's life? The answer would probably have been no. But since Russell was already dead and there was nothing I could do to bring him back, I answered that I hoped all the good that could possibly come from his death *would* come from it. If Russell's death could help improve someone else's life, stranger or no, I hoped it would.

I know Russell's death doesn't ensure anything, although I feel like it should. I'm still here, which means I still have tests and trials to endure well before I can be assured of anything. My children can still—and probably will—make bad choices. It's not certain that all of my family members will stay close to the gospel even after experiencing Russell's death. Many strangers will still avoid God even after hearing Russell's story. It is a terrible reality that I have no control over. I can't change anyone's use of agency but mine. And if I want Russell's death to mean anything or have the potential to save others, I have to be willing to put forth the effort necessary to make it meaningful.

I realized that my actions and responses to this situation could either help or hinder the possible good that could come from Russell's death and that I needed to do the best *I* could to make sure all the good that could come from Russell's death would come. It scared me to feel the power I had for good or bad. I could take this painfully debilitating, crushing blow and become bitter and drag people down with me. Or I could remember the sacred, hallowed experience of being in the Savior's presence and help lift others to that plane. I could tear down, or I could build up. I had a responsibility. But I could barely move. Even breathing was excruciating. I did not know if I would survive to the next minute! But I could make a conscious choice to make Russell's death matter—to reach out when I could and especially when I *had* to—no matter how scary or painful it might be. Luckily, throughout the coming days and weeks we had many people willing to reach out to show us how. They became my examples of what I was now called to do.

A local couple who had heard our story came to visit. They had lost their six-year-old son two months before and had come to share our anguish. We were touched at their thoughtfulness when they were obviously still in so much pain themselves. I was surprised by how apparent their grief still was. They gave us pointers for planning a funeral and shared things that had worked well and not so well for them. It was comforting to have that kind of information from people who, like us, had learned the hard way.

I found comfort in such information and hungered for more, and so I turned to modern scripture. I *love* listening to general conference every six months. I love listening to the familiar voices of leaders who feel like dear friends to me. I have a collection of super-favorite talks I want to remember. Sometimes, when I am especially empty, I pull out old *Ensign* magazines and refill myself on past conference talks. They always manage to give me the lift and encouragement I need. I looked for the conference talk that had been in my mind since that moment in the emergency room when I'd had my "but if not" moment. I did not know the speaker's name; I just figured the talk might be entitled "But if Not." I had a strong desire to hear it again, to gain strength from it that I hadn't gained the first time.

I asked my sister to look it up for me. She found "But if Not," by Elder Lance B. Wickman from the October 2002 general conference.[3] As I began to read, I realized it was not the talk I had been thinking of; I didn't remember ever hearing this one.

But in this talk, Elder Wickman describes the experience of losing his five-year-old son, Adam. Like me, Elder Wickman felt the overwhelming presence of the Savior in the hospital room as he pled for the life of his son. He talks of accepting the Lord's will for his family, of lessons learned through that trial. As I read this talk five and a half years after it was written, I felt like it had been written just for me. It was more than serendipitous that this talk had the same title as the one I felt inspired to read.

Later, I was able to track down the other conference talk. Similarly, it was entitled "But if Not . . ." by Elder Dennis E. Simmons from the April

2004 general conference.[4] In it, Elder Simmons talks of faith and of the tests we must endure in this life and the "but if not" moments we may be called upon to live through. Reading this talk made me smile. I felt like I was getting a hug from an old friend.

Back with the family, we started to plan the funeral. What songs did we want sung and by whom? Who would tell Russell's life sketch? How could we incorporate the cousins, the aunts, and the uncles as well as the grandparents so that everyone would have an opportunity to say good-bye? There were special friends and Russell's Sunbeam teacher we also wanted to include. It was a monumental task to perform in a short amount of time.

So among the tears, the hugs, and the heavy fog of grief, we began to pack up our things and prepare to return to a home without Russell.

## Chapter Three
### WHAT SAVED ME

THE OTHER DAYS FOLLOWING RUSSELL'S death are a blur to me, the details vague. But there are things I will never forget. While we were still in Utah, we had to figure out how to get Russell and the rest of our family home. We had to make some pretty significant decisions, and it was a struggle given the stupor we were in.

Kirk's boss offered to fly us home commercially, and my parents and siblings were checking all of their frequent flyer miles to see if they had enough to fly all of us home. David's brother John offered to pay for a private jet. He had been so generous already that we did not want to take advantage of his offer, but when we found out that Russell could fly with us on the jet, we decided we couldn't say no. David, John, and another friend drove our cars all the way home for us. They made the barest number of pit stops and drove all night so they could meet us at the airport in Orange County and fly home on the jet. I was amazed by their generosity and willingness to do that for us. I had no way to thank them enough. I could barely string two words together at that point, but I felt a deep sense of gratitude for all their kindness.

I am one of *those* Mormon women—one who's self-sufficient. You know our type: we can do it all, and even when we can't, we don't ask for help. I usually can't do it all very well, but I pride myself on the fact that I still can do it. After Russell died, I could not do much except sit and stare out the window at nothing. It was hard to focus. It was hard to complete a thought, let alone a complete sentence. I felt like I was suffocating under the enormity of what had to be done. My can-do attitude kept telling me to do *something*, yet I was paralyzed by my grief. I was surprised at all of the people around me who were able to move and get things done. I was in a fog, moving slothlike, while it seemed everyone else was able to spring into action.

The plan was for us to fly into Long Beach Airport the next morning, where my family and some ward members would be waiting to pick us up. I honestly don't know who planned it all. I was either at the mortuary or sitting on the floor at John's house, my eyes staring vacantly, when it all got worked out. And somehow it *was* all worked out. Enough drivers agreed to come; we just had to show up.

Before we left Utah, we all drove to the mortuary, where we had a special prayer with Russell's little body present. We also wanted to make sure the mortuary sent the right casket to put on the plane. Since federal law does not allow the opening of a casket outside, we had to make sure it was the right one before we got to the airport. I was worried, but I didn't need to be. Russell's casket was the smallest at the mortuary.

On the way to the airport, my mother-in-law turned around and said, "I've been up all night thinking about what you need to do for the funeral. The most important thing you need to do is get some nice tablecloths from the Relief Society and get tables set up. You need to make a nice display of Russell's life with pictures and toys and special things he liked. This way, everyone who comes to the funeral will feel like they know and understand what a sweet and fun boy Russell was."

That comment struck terror in my heart and completely overwhelmed me. I am not a "pretty display" kind of person. Whenever I'd taught Relief Society, I felt accomplished if I remembered to bring something to slap down on the table before my lesson. I don't do scrapbooks, and I don't know how to make an area look pretty. Now I was being given the great responsibility of introducing my dead son to hundreds of people who didn't know him well. I understood the enormity and importance of this task; I just didn't think I was able to do Russell justice. I pondered and fretted about this the entire way home.

When we got home, there was a note taped to our front door. It said simply,

*Jenny, I am so sorry for your loss. I want to help you, but I don't want to step on any toes. Could I do Russell's tables for the funeral?*
—*Geralene*

That small note felt like it had fluttered straight down from heaven and answered my unspoken prayer. Geralene and a few others came to my house and picked out things they thought would be a good representation of Russell. They planned out what they would need and made specific requests of what I could gather for them. I can't explain how much this eased my apprehension about setting the tone for the funeral. This I could do. I could find Russell's favorite toys, blankets, and dress-ups. Every time Geralene came over, I talked about the items I gave her—I especially like talking about Russell's superhero toys. We were able to laugh and cry as we remembered funny times. Talking about Russell was a blessing.

Along with the note on the door, we found four humongous stuffed animals on our doorstep. Each was addressed to one of my living children with the note "I have a hug for you whenever you need it." These animals got hugs right there on the doorstep.

When we walked into our house, we were bowled over by the amount of food on the table. There was no room left in the refrigerator or cupboards. We had left for Utah with a minimal amount of food in the fridge, knowing that we were going to be gone so long and that it probably wouldn't last. We were blessed to find everything restocked—even a burned-out light in the kitchen was replaced! Even more amazing, someone had left a detailed list of all the food that had been given to us and a page of menu ideas. In my bewildered state, I couldn't concentrate or think straight. If someone had said, "I'm hungry," I would have looked at all that food and not been able to do a thing with any of it. Now I had the tools and didn't have to *think*.

Along with the food, a sister in our ward gave us a basket to put the hundreds and hundreds of cards we'd received in and a notebook to write down the things people were doing for us. I was so busy planning for the funeral and so overcome with emotion I couldn't read the cards. But I put them in the basket, knowing I'd be able to get to them later. The notebook was like gold. I wrote down addresses I didn't have and notes of special things people did for us and made lists of things I needed to do. After the funeral, I sent DVDs of it to family members unable to come. I made a list of everyone who needed one and crossed it off after I mailed it. A week or so later, I couldn't remember if I had sent a DVD to one of my aunts. I consulted my list. There was her name, crossed off. My memory was so fuzzy and spotty that without the notebook, I would have been lost.

My parents and brother and sister-in-law came and did all our trip laundry, cleaned the house (no easy task), and put the Christmas decorations away. Then my parents took the children to their house for a few days while Kirk and I managed the tasks of preparing for the funeral, dressing Russell's body, and finding a cemetery plot. I had no idea how much time and work went into planning a funeral—and what a challenge those things are when you can hardly function.

That first night home, I remember crawling into bed and finding that someone had put cozy flannel sheets on it. It felt so warm and comfortable; for the first time since Russell's death, I felt secure and safe. Although my sleep was fleeting and sporadic, I enjoyed the warmth and protection of my bed. For the next few weeks I was constantly bone cold and uncomfortable. It was nice to be able to snuggle into my bed—even though I knew sleep would not come easily—and feel a small escape of some sort. I still don't know who put those sheets on my bed. They probably didn't know such a small thing would be such a saving grace to me.

Our family was being sheltered during that first week home. The bishopric and Relief Society sent e-mails to everyone with the details of what had happened and a request to not call or visit for a few days while we got our bearings. But that didn't stop people from caring. Neighborhood children drew pictures of Russell for us. A friend asked if she could make a digital slideshow of Russell. Many unknown angels developed our digital pictures so they could be displayed at the funeral. Sign-ups went around for people to bring us dinners for the entire month of January. So many people wanted to help that we had breakfast, lunch, and snack foods brought in weekly for the kids.

As a mother of five, I know how nice it is to have a few dinners brought in when a baby is born. It's nice not to have to plan a meal and get up to make it with a new baby. But when a child dies, making dinner is not just hard; it's almost impossible. I was not functioning. I was not attentive. I was physically unable to prepare anything more complicated than cold cereal. Our ward saved us from my inability to move. I couldn't go to the store or make decisions, not even about what kind of peanut butter to buy.

The first time I went to Target with the kids, just to exchange a movie, I had a panic attack. I found myself randomly walking the aisles at the grocery store—and crying uncontrollably and bolting for the door. Clearly, I didn't have the energy for the simplest of everyday tasks. I was grateful my ward and neighborhood friends allowed me to stay inside my little cocoon and hibernate for a season.

Although the ward did their best not to impose, we had a few friends sneak through the firing lines. Because their visits weren't overwhelming, they were like a breath of fresh air. I can't even remember who all came over, but I do remember laughing as they shared funny memories. Some memories were about Russell, and some weren't. Some of these friends knew Russell well, and some barely knew him at all. That part didn't seem to be important. We knew they loved us, that they hurt for us, and that their visits gave us a break from our grief.

It seemed everyone wanted to help. Bringing food was not enough. A friend jumped at the opportunity when I needed someone to get balloons for the dedication of the grave. I only had to ask one person for each thing I needed, and I watched my seemingly endless list of things to do become smaller and smaller.

Since superheroes were such a big part of Russell's life, we wanted the pallbearers and friends and family to wear superhero ties at the funeral. Actually, I wanted them to wear superhero costumes in honor of Russell, but Kirk said no. I can't remember whom I asked to find the ties; I just remember how sad she was when she got back to me, telling me she'd been all over town and on the Internet looking for ties. Apparently there wasn't a huge market for superhero ties because there weren't enough for the funeral.

Hearing of our plight, a group of ladies from my mom's ward stepped in. I'd known these ladies growing up—some were old Young Women leaders and others just my mom's friends. They found cute Spider-Man material and a tie pattern and went to town. They made enough ties—and hair scrunchies!—for anyone associated with the funeral and gave us extra to hand out. They spent many long nights to get this project done just so that the funeral could be that much more meaningful.

I was sad most of the time, but I was still full of hope. Even though we felt shock, loneliness, and a deep sense of loss, the special experience Kirk and I had had at the hospital enabled me to see beyond the dark clouds obscuring my view and occasionally get a glimpse of eternity. I found myself lifting others and explaining the beauties of the gospel to them. I could comfort those who could not understand how a loving Father would allow such a tragedy. I was able to see that our loss was not a tragedy but would one day be looked upon as a blessing. Of course, that day would be after my own death, when I would be able to sit with Russell in heaven and look over how my life was affected by his passing through the veil.

I later realized that this optimism was due in part to the faith of the friends, family, and ward members praying and fasting for my family. I've prayed and fasted for many people in my life, and I've had people pray for me during hardships before, but never have I experienced the tangible buffer I felt those few weeks after Russell died. I was buoyed up in a very real and physical sense. I felt I could almost touch the protective bubble surrounding me. The small though inestimably significant prayers of my angels on earth helped carry me through what surely would have been a harder time without them and kept me looking heavenward. Over time, I could actually feel the prayers diminishing and lessening; it was as if I was slowly being released from the protective hands of my Father in Heaven and placed into regular earth life again.

One of my greatest fears at this time was that I would forget all of my memories and unique stories about Russell. It was so hard to think. Much like the night we'd gone to bed on that fateful day, I could not picture him alive and happy. When I closed my eyes, he was cold and still, his skin almost transparent white. My memories were jumbled and fragmented. It was an awful feeling to have lost Russell physically and then to have my memories of him slowly being pulled away, just beyond my grasp. I wanted pictures and memories compiled and documented—solid proof that he had been real and not just a ghost in my mind. I wanted all of his friends' and my friends' memories of him written down before they too forgot.

I was just so tired and busy, overwhelmed, and unsure how to go about collecting it all before it got lost in the recesses of our brains. Unbeknownst to me, a friend did what I was unable to. She called and e-mailed, collected and compiled. She set up scrapbooking nights where women got together and scrapped the night away.

Remember, I am not a scrapbooker. In my wildest dreams I imagined a nice little scrapbook of Russell, but realistically, I just hoped to have some random memories written down on lined paper. What I got far surpassed my wildest imagination. I got a *huge* scrapbook filled with specific memories and impressions of Russell, complete with pictures, stickers, and all the fixings. And if that wasn't enough, they also presented me with another *huge* scrapbook of just pictures. Most of the images I had never seen—preschool, nursery, photos from someone's birthday party, a park day. It was such a treat to see my little guy in a different light. In a large way, these gifts helped reclaim my memories and calm my troubled mind.

The young women in the ward graciously offered to babysit for members of my family and anyone participating in the funeral both during the viewing and the funeral. This was extremely helpful since there were quite a few small children. At the viewing, Kirk and I couldn't keep an eye on our own kids, and we didn't want to worry about them wandering the halls or running around. I wanted to soak in the entire day. It may sound absurd, but it was, for me, the happiest day since Russell had died. For those few short hours, I felt Russell's spirit close by. My family was all together again, and I knew this would be one of the last times I would feel that completeness for a long, long time. I would not have been able to drink in the experience with a wiggly, whiney one-and-a-half-year-old. Besides, I did not have the energy to contain or control any of my kids.

My neighbors and many women—and probably men, but I wasn't paying attention—served my family a luncheon after the graveside service. It was a great opportunity for my neighbors, whom I had invited many times to come to Church activities, to see how we members helped each other. They spent time in the building getting to know other Latter-day Saints and see them being charitable to my family. Although none of them is ready to be baptized, they got to see a different side of how Mormons live. I imagine they see me going to church with my family for three long hours every Sunday, heading off to various meetings and activities, or leaving the house with dinner for someone else and probably think I spend too much time with my religion. This time they were able to feel the reward of charitable service. It was a wonderful opportunity, and I think it brought a little more light into their lives.

Amazingly, my children's current and previous schoolteachers and administrators attended the funeral and graveside services. My children were worried about going back to school. They didn't want to talk about how their brother died. They didn't want to be the center of attention because of *this*. They wanted to slide back into school undetected and have things magically go back to normal. I had talked to the teachers and told them of my children's concerns. After the funeral, their current teachers handed me a folder full of letters from each of the kids' classmates.

Some said sweet things like, "I'm sorry your brother died." But for my children, the letters they really valued said things like, "I hope you come back to school soon. I miss you." These letters were a gift from heaven to my kids. It gave them the confidence and the courage to return to school, to face the unknown and make it their own. These insightful teachers were angels to me because they helped my children make it through what would have been an otherwise nearly impossible transition, and I will be forever grateful.

My friend Geralene was never afraid to ask questions, and so she knew I was worried about the kids' memories of Russell fading. Ever thoughtful and supportive, she found the cutest cube frames for each of my kids and put pictures of each sibling with Russell in them. What a gift to my kids! Each of them has their cube somewhere in their room, and they look at it often.

*  *  *

In the weeks and months after the funeral, I wanted to make sense of all the madness inside me. As a result of what I had experienced at the hospital, I knew Russell's death was part of a plan, but I was now so sad. Don't get me wrong, I *expected* to be sad, but this was so much worse than I dreamed. My heart felt like it was going to explode. It hurt to breathe. It *physically* hurt to inhale. A constant pressure on my chest made me feel as if my ribs were constricting my lungs. No matter if I was standing, sitting, lying down, or on my head, it was a never-ending battle as I struggled to keep breathing.

I experienced my first panic attack the day after Russell died. I experienced many more—and many far more severe—after that. My mind became befuddled. I struggled to think, to formulate simple sentences. I had a hard time concentrating or communicating and often asked others to repeat themselves. I couldn't follow conversations that moved quickly. Television was out of the question. I felt myself getting smaller and smaller, more isolated, as I avoided painful memories and situations.

I hated meeting new people, especially random strangers I'd never see again. I became a recluse when taking Joey to the park. When other moms smiled and said hello, I stared vacantly at them while trying desperately to remember proper social etiquette. I felt abnormal, freakish. I just could not remember what normal behavior was. I would say things to other moms, see their shocked expressions, and only then realize I'd said something inappropriate. I was constantly second-guessing myself.

When trapped in a conversation with someone who didn't know my history, I always tried to stay one step ahead. I purposely asked them *anything* except how many children they had because if I did, they would inevitably repeat the question back to me. I could not bear to answer it. I tried to anticipate their questions and answers while steering them away from subjects involving their—and my—children. It was exhausting. When one mom talks to another for the first time, they invariably ask about each other's kids. It's only natural. It's almost a law. But I couldn't do it. I couldn't ask because I couldn't tell. So I avoided situations where I would meet new people.

I practiced saying, "I had a son named Russell who was almost five, but he died this year." I practiced saying it aloud whenever I was alone. I thought it in my head whenever I talked to new people who couldn't have known. But most of the time I chickened out and never said it. I wasn't ready to say it to someone else. Although just practicing and hearing the words was helpful, I think, in the realization and acceptance of it.

Eventually I could say the words to others, but I still don't tell everyone I meet. Now, when asked how many children I have, I say five. When asked their ages—naturally the next question—I say, "My oldest is sixteen, and my youngest is six." That's usually enough to move the conversation forward. If they persist, they get the ugly truth and have to decide how to react when they hear it.

After a time, I started practicing answers to other hard questions. If I had an answer ready, I felt more in control, more confident. I practiced my answers aloud in the car, in front of my mirror, and whenever I was alone. It was something I needed to do to help reintroduce myself to society. I knew I could hide, isolating myself forever. And although I still do that sometimes when it gets dark and again I struggle to breathe and cope, I don't want to lose my place in society. I like the closeness of others. I need friendships and the strength I glean from those around me. Slowly, and after many clumsy attempts, I was able to come back from my long journey. Although I will never be the same, I have been welcomed back by those who helped me return. Their love, support, guidance, and prayers helped to save my life, and I will forever be in their debt.

* * *

Physically, I was in pretty good shape when Russell died. I ran almost every day and flirted with the idea of entering some ultra-type races. After Russell died, I was too busy to exercise at first. I wasn't eating or sleeping much and, not surprisingly, didn't have the energy to work out. I knew this could be a turning point in the way I exercised in the future and that if I gave up running, I would be zapped of my strength and the will to move. All the books said that exercise helped with depression, so I knew I should continue with some semblance of my previous regimen. I felt that if I got out of the habit now, I might never get back into it. The problem was, I could not run by myself. I had so many negative thoughts swirling through my brain that it was not healthy for me to be alone. I could control the thoughts if I ran with Joey in the stroller, but it just seemed like too much work. I wondered what I was going to do but didn't feel the need to make a decision and act on it.

The week after the funeral, a sister from my ward named Tania came to pay her respects. At the time, I didn't know Tania well, but I had always admired her. I had become acquainted with her through my sister-in-law Karina when they were in the same ward. We talked for a little while, getting to know each other better. We both bemoaned the fact that Karina had moved. Tania missed running with Karina and asked if I would be interested in taking Karina's place as her running partner. Tania tried to tell me how much it would help and motivate *her* if we ran together, but I saw through the flimsy ruse: she was there, sitting in front of me, blatantly answering another unspoken prayer. Tania will never understand or know how much I needed someone to run with. I didn't really understand or know how important our partnership was until many months later.

Mornings were my most challenging time of day. In the fragile moments between dreaming and wakefulness, I could almost convince myself that it had all been a bad dream. As my consciousness became more alert, I would realize by degrees the reality of my situation: my son was dead, and it would be years—my entire lifetime—before I would hold him and talk to him again. My chest would tighten, tears would stream down my face, and the sadness would set in. I would bury my face in my pillow, trying to reclaim the magic I had felt just minutes before. Then the realization would hit that I had to get out of bed, get the children ready for school, make lunches, do laundry, wash the dishes, and resume my regular responsibilities. It all felt too heavy to bear.

Other mornings, or in the middle of the night, I woke from nightmares so ghoulish and terrifying it would take me hours to calm down. I have seen Russell's death many times in my dreams. Other nights, I've watched each of my other children die, with me helpless to save them. I wasn't sleeping much anyway, but on the days after such nightmares, I was more frazzled and on edge, with a pit in my stomach and a hole in my heart. Most mornings I simply fought getting out of bed. However, I found that on the mornings I ran with Tania, I woke up immediately, jumped out of bed, and was ready before she showed up at my door.

We met in the dark, at the ghastly early-morning seminary hour, and ran the forty-five minutes her children were at the church. It seemed I got even less sleep than before, but I felt more refreshed and had more energy than if I'd stayed in bed listening to my demons. I wasn't feeling the usual "runner's high" I had previously enjoyed after a good run, and I wondered how effective our runs actually were. But I enjoyed our conversation. It was therapeutic to talk out my problems and listen to Tania's.

We ran together every few days the remainder of the school year. By summer, it was too hard and too hot to schedule running time together. But by then I was more comfortable in my skin, and I could tolerate short runs alone. Some of them still ended in panic attacks or tears, but for the most part I was able to exercise without Tania. When it got just too hot to run at all, I gave it up for a week. A surprising thing happened. My depression, which would come in waves, now threatened to engulf me. I still hadn't experienced the "runner's high," but now I found that all of that running with Tania had protected me from deeper and more brutal lows. The physical effects of our exercise together was yet one more blessing from that day when yet another angel had listened to the promptings of the Spirit.

* * *

There were so many people who wanted to help us, to ease our pain and lift our grief. Friends and strangers alike were creative in the unique ways they reached out to us.

I was in a dinner group, which meant that once a week I cooked for four other families. On the other weekdays, meals from the other families in the group came to us. It was a time-saver, but that one cooking day was usually stressful and chaotic. As the month of meals graciously provided by the ward came to a close, I tried to gear up for cooking again. I wasn't sure if I could cook for four families, but I didn't want to quit the dinner group. A sister in my ward who was not a member of our group offered not only to make the dinners for my night that first week back, but she also brought snuggly fleece blankets she'd made for each of my kids. I don't like to cook—which was why I was in the dinner group in the first place—and was amazed that someone would offer to make all that food for me. Such an unusual and heartfelt gift gave me one more week to become stronger as the days following the funeral stretched endlessly before me.

Every day was emotional, but I soon found Sundays to be the worst in that respect. I'd start the morning listening to Church songs in an attempt to keep a spirit of reverence in our boisterous house, where chaotic morning scenes of trying to get everyone ready and out the door at a reasonable time were the norm. Once at church, I felt sustained and uplifted by our friends there.

The songs though—they affected me the most. I had loved singing before the accident. I had a decent voice and was in the choir. It was my time to praise my Heavenly Father. A song in my heart or on my lips really did feel like a prayer to me. But right after Russell died, I could not sing.

First it was because I had a cold and had cried so much my voice was hoarse. Just looking at the words or thinking them was enough. When I was able to sing the songs in sacrament meeting, I was overcome with emotion. I couldn't sing at all anymore. Not Church songs, not with the radio. I hadn't realized that actually singing a song created a much deeper connection between me and the meaning of the song. All of a sudden, I had begun to feel the great love my Heavenly Father had for me by letting His Son die. I felt His pain as I sang the hymn before the sacrament. I felt the Savior's sadness and grief when we sang about His suffering in the Garden of Gethsemane. I began to feel the joy of the gospel more deeply. The songs that were so meaningful and special to me before became so much more meaningful that I felt I was learning things for the first time, every time I sang a hymn.

By the end of sacrament meeting I was usually a wet, blubbery mess. I was self-conscious about it because I had previously had a pretty good handle on my emotions. I noticed people avoiding me in the halls. I didn't blame them. I even saw a friend look at me then quickly turn around so she didn't have to talk to me. It was an awkward attempt to escape on her part because it was pretty obvious she was avoiding me. Quite a few people wouldn't meet my gaze or make eye contact—even when talking to me.

I have been on that side of life, and I remember how scary it can be to talk to someone who is going through a hard time. You want to say just the right thing, but what if you don't and you make them cry or make it worse? What if you say something stupid or offensive by accident? Even with all of the experience I now have with the loss of a loved one, I still have the same insecurities when talking to someone else who has also suffered a loss. Back when the wound was fresh, I tried not to be offended or feel rebuffed. I wasn't surprised by their reactions because I understood how they were feeling.

What did surprise me, though, were the people who went out of their way to talk to me. We were still a new ward, barely a year old. I had tried to get to know everyone, although several members I still only knew by name. It was these people who amazed me the most. People I barely knew had the courage to say hello. Ward members I'd never really talked to made the effort to come up and chat with me. They said encouraging things to me like, "I enjoyed your testimony," or, "I've been thinking about you this week." I was touched at their willingness to break out of their comfort zones to offer me support.

One family moved into the ward after Kirk became bishop. The wife was a younger woman with younger children. We talked a few times, and she seemed comfortable around me. But when she found out I was the bishop's wife, all that changed. She was suddenly intimidated and nervous around me. I still tried to talk to her, but our conversations never seemed to last long. After Russell died, I figured she would never have the nerve to talk to me again.

However, about a month after his death, this sister came up to the piano while I was playing prelude music in Primary. She stood there for a minute, not sure what to say. I'm not a good piano player, so I was unable to look up or say anything with more than one syllable.

Finally she said, "Hi, Sister Hess." She still had a hard time calling me Jenny. "I've been thinking about you. How are you doing?" Then she began verbally berating herself. "Oh my gosh. I have been working up the nerve to talk to you for a month, and that's the first thing I say?" Then she ran out of the room. I was still playing and couldn't run after her.

What she didn't know was that while I could tell how hard it had been for her, I felt an incredible outpouring of love and tenderness as she stood nervously beside me. When she'd asked how I was doing, I felt her concern and smiled. When she quickly left, I actually laughed. I wasn't laughing at *her* but at the scene. She had given me a beautiful feeling inside that made me so happy I laughed. It was the first time I had felt that way in a long time, and it has lasted in my heart to this day.

I was getting used to being talked to in whispers and hushed tones. I was getting used to being handled with kid gloves. People were careful with me, and I was starting to feel like I was made of glass and could break at any time. Which is why Dave, a robust, energetic man in our ward, was so refreshing. He would have none of it. "Hi, Jenny!" his voice boomed across the chapel before church each Sunday. "Good to see you!"

I had chatted with Dave occasionally before Russell died, but it seemed to me that he sought me out every Sunday for several months just to say hello. He made eye contact. He made sure everyone heard him talking to me. He actually smiled at me with a real smile—not that sad, "I'm so sorry for your loss" kind of smile I was so used to. Dave brought me back to the land of the living. He made me feel normal at a time when I felt uncomfortably abnormal. He helped me believe I was made of hardy plastic, not glass, and that I would not break if I fell. Dave gave me the confidence to talk to people who were afraid to talk to me.

* * *

Angels both inside the Church and outside of it made the weeks and months following Russell's death bearable with their kind and thoughtful deeds. One of Kirk's counselors conducted the funeral and helped organize all the forces. I know he did much, much more than that, but he did it all quietly behind the scenes. His wife spent hours visiting me and crying with me on the phone and at the park and at my house.

One friend called or came by at the beginning of every month to let me know she was thinking about me. Sometimes she brought a little something for the family. Long after others stopped associating the first of every month with the day Russell died and after most visitors, phone calls, and cards stopped coming, this sweet lady still came. The fact that I knew she was still thinking of me strengthened me on especially bad days.

Still another friend called to check up on me often. She wrote a beautiful poem about Russell and included a picture of him running, which we hung on the wall. On what would have been Russell's first day of kindergarten, this friend became my buffer. She recognized how painful it would be for me and went to school with me and the other kids. I felt protected and accepted, even though I had a hard time holding it together as I watched the other parents take pictures and hug their kindergarteners.

One dear woman offered to watch Joey once a week. It took me more than ten months to take her up on it. I was just not ready to be alone. My friend patiently waited until I was able, then she watched him one day a week for almost a year. I used that quiet time to write my "Russell book"—a biography of his life and all the fun memories I had of him. It took me over a year to complete, but without this friend's invaluable help, it wouldn't have happened. Often she can tell when I'm struggling and she's not afraid to let me cry—because sometimes I need to. We've spent many afternoons together doing just that: crying. I learned that crying with someone is usually way better than crying alone.

A new sister moved into the ward several months after Russell died. She'd never met him, but when she heard our story, she tried to find something meaningful to do for us. She knew that Kirk's calling kept him busy, especially nights after work, and so she asked if she could come over once a week to just help out.

I've already noted that I'm one of "those" Mormon women who thinks she can do it all by herself. I wouldn't let this sister do my dishes or clean my house. So we just chatted. We got to know each other and learned from each other. She listened to me talk endlessly about a little boy she would never meet in this lifetime, and she never seemed bored. For the first few months I did most of the talking. Later, I was able to listen. It was good for me to hear about her problems, to see that even though I was in pain, life was bigger than the death of my son. Imagine our surprise when we realized it had been a year since her first visit! I wondered that someone would give up that much time for me—almost weekly visits for an entire year!

Most of the angels in my life are living, breathing, hardworking, busy people who have taken time out of their lives to give me something I couldn't get for myself. I am indebted to them and hold the deepest gratitude for them. I am convinced that my Eternal Father is grateful to them too. He is the greatest Paymaster, and they have put themselves on His payroll through their thoughtful actions toward me. They saved me at a time when I was drowning in grief and pain and could not save myself. I will never be able to pay them back for the goodness I was given. I can only hope to pay it forward and be an angel to someone else in their great time of need.

## *Chapter Four*
### LIVING TOGETHER, GRIEVING APART

A MONTH OR TWO AFTER Russell died, I took one of the children to the doctor. The nurse, who knew about the situation, asked how Kirk and I were holding up. I'm sure I told her we were doing our best to survive. Her reply surprised me: "At least you guys have each other and are able to grieve together."

Grieve *together*? I was surprised she'd phrased it that way. It sounded ludicrous to me at the time. Kirk was a man and grieved like a man—stoic, brave, and without much emotion that I could see. I was a woman and grieved like a woman—crying almost all of the time and unable to cope.

Now, years later, our grief is not as raw, and it has lessened in intensity. We are still grieving, and we still grieve differently. We are both more stable in our grief, but we still address things like anniversaries and holidays differently.

I imagined the nurse had some romantic notion of Kirk and I clinging to each other, weeping together for the loss of our son. If I'd ever given thought to a couple losing a child, I would have had that same notion: couples arm in arm, talking through their feelings and holding each other.

Reality for me has been the complete opposite.

As I mentioned before, even that first night, Kirk lay silent on one side of the bed while I lay silent on the other. We were each caught up in our own thoughts, memories, and sense of denial and shock at what had happened. We were both replaying the awful scenes we'd witnessed at the hospital, trying to make sense of it all in our own ways.

And yes, every once in a while, when it became too much for one person to handle, we did reach out for one another and sob. But then, without speaking, we retreated again to our silent reveries.

As soon as we came home from the trip, there was so much to be done, even with my parents taking care of the children so we could do it all without interruption. And yet, in spite of our to-do lists, we often wandered aimlessly around the house.

Kirk withdrew to his office, where he painstakingly compiled every picture we had of Russell. He'd bought our first digital camera the day Russell was born. We had no idea at the time what an inspired purchase it had been. Every year since then, Kirk had organized the pictures into files—each holiday, each family trip, and each individual had their own file. We'd taken thousands of pictures in about five years. Kirk went through them all.

I'm sure it was an emotionally draining process for him. I asked if he needed help. He said no, and I didn't press it. I assumed it was something he needed to do alone, and, frankly, I couldn't bear to look at all those pictures of Russell smiling at me. Not yet.

After going through the pictures, Kirk spent days working on his funeral talk. We tend to be private when writing talks, not bouncing ideas off each other or practicing in front of each other. This was no exception. I had no idea what Kirk was going to say at the funeral, what direction he was going to go. I don't think even he knew for a while.

One day he said, "I'm not sure my talk will all come together, and even if it does, I'm not sure I'll be able to deliver it."

"Have someone else do it," I kept telling him. He didn't need the heavy responsibility. But Kirk felt compelled, almost driven, to speak at the funeral.

I could accept that because I'd begun writing voraciously. I felt like I had to write out our trip, to chronicle the accident and include every minute detail. I had all these memories swirling around my brain. Feeling like a demon possessed, I wrote like crazy to get it out, as if putting the painful memories into words could somehow take them away. Perhaps putting it all on paper would force the trauma from my brain, give it another place to live.

Unfortunately that was not the case. The pain stayed, but writing did help; I felt some measure of peace and satisfaction in recording it all. Instead of the memories infecting every part of my brain, I now had a small closet space in my mind free of the monsters that had lurked there. It was where I put my happy memories of Russell and our family times together. When the pain and devastation became too much, I opened the closet door to visit.

After writing down every last memory about our trip and Russell's accident, I shut my journal. I paper clipped those pages together so I wouldn't accidentally open to them. Those pages had been unmercifully loud as I'd written them, screaming, demanding to be heard. I'd felt the compulsion to write the words. I had no desire to *read* them.

I did not notice Kirk's absence as I wrote, nor did he notice mine while he wrote. We weren't in the same room, and, looking back, it is hard to believe we were even in the same galaxy. We were each absorbed in our own task, oblivious to our surroundings. Occasionally we took breaks and staggered out of our rooms, rubbing our eyes with wonder. Where were we? Why was it so quiet?

We talked then, in whispers, Kirk of his inability to express what he wanted in his talk and I of a letter I was writing to the ER doctors. We discussed the next phase of planning for the funeral—dressing Russell's body, visiting the cemetery to pick a plot, deciding on other speakers and songs, which pictures to use for the funeral program. There was so much to do. Yet we could not move. We were lost in our own thoughts. Separate, yet side by side.

We did what we could together, but we still did much alone. At night we held each other but barely talked. That worked for us. We both instinctively knew that we each had to deal with things our own ways. That's how it felt; I did what I needed to do, and he did what he needed to—alone and separate—but then we periodically checked up on each other to reconnect.

We talked, but the house was *very* quiet those first few days. Gradually we began talking again of regular things. We still had living children and daily tasks to take care of, even while we were grieving. I could have been angry at the way Kirk expressed his grief, but I wasn't. I understood that we each needed to express the grief our own ways. Kirk understood this as well.

After the children came back from my parents' house, we realized that children grieve differently than adults. The house would be somber and quiet one minute, and then the children would be wrestling on the floor. Sometimes they would be laughing while they were all tangled up, and sometimes they would be yelling and blaming each other and tattling loudly.

It is completely normal for children who are grieving to "take a break" from their grief. When their brains can't absorb any more sadness and things become too intense, they have the ability to simply turn it off for a while and fall back into their habitual, everyday routines. I'm sure it's some kind of primal survival mechanism that helps them live through this kind of pain, but it is challenging for adults to accept this kind of behavior as grieving. There are times when it appears that children aren't grieving at all. But it doesn't mean they aren't hurting or that they don't love the one they've lost. Children who can take a break from their overwhelming emotions and not be pulled down in endless depression end up healing more rapidly than those who grieve like little adults.

While I was glad that my children were able to grieve in a healthy manner, I was frustrated at times with their frivolity. They could laugh and play as if nothing was wrong. They could fight and argue as if our family was normal. They could think about the mundane and expect me to answer their silly questions as if I was not broken.

I reminded myself to be thankful when our house was noisy and full of chaos, even though I would have preferred it to be solemn and subdued. I tried to match their enthusiasm about an upcoming activity. I tried to smile when they told me about some exciting event in their day. I tried not to yell and tirade when they were having too much fun. I knew they loved and missed Russell, even when they didn't show it in the way I would have preferred.

The children decided to go back to school two days after the funeral. Kirk went back to work and resumed his duties as bishop. I woke up early almost every morning before the family got up to run with Tania. That way I was up to help the children get ready for school. I got them off every day then came back to my near-empty house. Then I usually just cried. If it hadn't been for twenty-one-month-old Joey, I would have gone back to bed.

Not that I was accomplishing much; I did the bare minimum with Joey. Luckily, he let me know when he was hungry—I might have forgotten to feed him otherwise. As it was, Joey was a patient, albeit demanding, teacher. He let me know exactly what he needed every minute of the day. He put up with my tears and lethargy as long as I met his demands. Mostly he demanded that I hold him a lot and keep him close—both of which I was more than willing to do.

Children are aware of the grieving cues set by their caregivers. Since overwhelming or debilitating grief can be scary for them to watch, I tried to hide these unsettling emotions from them. But children need to see that grief is a natural byproduct of loss. Everyone grieves in some way, and children need to observe healthy role models working through grief. When they see adults openly grieving, they learn that it is okay to cry and acknowledge that they miss the one they are grieving for.

I didn't show my children all my grief though. I kept many of the new anxieties and panic attacks I experienced inside my head. These new emotions were terrifying to experience, and I didn't want to burden my children with them. I did my best to spend my worst days alone or to hide my feelings of desolation. I tried to keep our schedule as normal as I could. I tried to be as normal as I could. I was there for my kids, giving them time, attention, and love. They had already lost a brother; I did not want them to think they had also lost their mother.

But my children saw me cry. They saw that I was sad. They also saw for the most part that I was able to get out of bed and be with them. They saw that their needs were still a priority to me, even if I couldn't meet them all as well as I used to.

Joey took my grieving in stride. He was too young to care if I was crying as long as I was holding him through my tears. Karissa, Kyle, and Jake were different. I noticed them staring quizzically at me at times as if they were trying to figure out the changes that were morphing me. Other times they would pointedly ignore me, giving me permission and space to grieve. I desperately wanted my children to get through this time of our lives unscathed. I didn't want to be the cause of any subconscious problems that could manifest later in their lives. I tried to grieve and cry as much as I could alone while letting them see it is natural to be sad and acceptable to cry. I tried to "check in" with them, to see how they were doing emotionally.

Although they didn't want to engage in conversations about their grief and their feelings, Karissa, Kyle, and Jake were more than willing to talk about Russell and their memories of him.

Karissa became more verbal. She included Russell in her prayers. She and I shared some tender moments talking about the accident and how we were dealing with it. Kyle was quiet about his grief, but he became more demonstrative in his affection for his siblings. He was more patient with his younger brothers and became a true friend to Karissa. Jake would sometimes "get something in his eyes" and need to go to the bathroom to get it out. He adamantly reminded us that he wasn't crying. But Jake mentioned Russell in our everyday conversations.

Joey didn't have the verbal skills yet and acted out his grief through crying, temper tantrums, and separation anxiety. Death was a concept he couldn't understand or make sense of and one I couldn't adequately explain. All he knew was his best friend had just disappeared. Russell was gone only a few hours a week at preschool, and he was home with Joey every other waking moment. They shared a room. He was always there. And then suddenly, he wasn't. And we couldn't tell Joey why.

We couldn't expect Joey to grieve as we grieved. He didn't want to be alone in a room, even when we were still in the house. When he was sad, he became inconsolable at times. He began hoarding toys, food, and any other precious commodity. His pockets were filled to overflowing with treasures he thought might disappear when he wasn't looking. He made hiding places for things that wouldn't fit in his arms or pockets. We found secret stashes all over the house and in the car.

Before long, I noticed that the older children slowly stopped talking as much about Russell. Their memories of him were fading.

And they were for me too. Specific memories seemed fleeting and sometimes hard to recall. But that's not to say I didn't think of Russell. He was always at the forefront of my mind. Before his death, he was with me the entire day except for the few hours of preschool. His absence left a huge hole in my life. Everywhere I looked I saw where he should have been—but wasn't. Everything I did or didn't do was a cruel reminder of my loss.

Before Russell died, every afternoon while Joey napped and the big children were at school, Russell and I would have our "Russell time." We read books, put puzzles together, colored pictures—whatever he chose. Now there was only silence where our laughter had been. Even setting the table for dinner was a torturous reminder that we were now a family of six, not seven. I felt the incalculable, deep, overwhelming, suffocating emptiness in every second of every day.

Before Russell died, I wasn't a very emotional person. I was generally happy and had trained myself to look for the good in any situation. I had survived many sad and traumatic events, but through each of them, I'd maintained my composure.

But Russell's death pierced me in a place I must have hidden so well I didn't even know it existed. No matter how hard I tried, I *couldn't* regain control or composure. Admittedly, I wasn't trying very hard; it took too much energy.

I tried to get most of my crying out while the older children were at school because my tears were hard on them. Sometimes I held it together when they got home, but sometimes six hours of crying wasn't enough. To cope, I talked to friends. I wrote in my journal. I pondered. I talked things over with God. Every once in a while I talked to Kirk about it.

Prior to Russell's death, I'd lived a typical life. I'd experienced the normal ups and downs of youth. I'd had hardships to overcome, but I'd had no experience with the sudden death of a loved one. Kirk, on the other hand, was already well acquainted with grief. When he was nine, his father, who we affectionately call Grandpa Kyle, died in a scuba-diving accident at a youth conference, leaving Kirk's mom alone, six months pregnant, with four young children. The accident was unexpected, shocking, sudden, but

Kirk's mom forged through. She learned many valuable lessons about life, death, loss, and endurance. She taught these lessons to her children, and she taught them well.

Kirk went back to work right away. At least in that way he was able to cope, to be normal. He seemed to have fallen back into a comfortable routine. Once, when we were "checking in" with one another, Kirk made the comment that he was surprised at how much I still cried. In thirteen and a half years of marriage, he'd never seen me like this.

*I* had never seen me like this! My emotions bewildered both of us, but I didn't understand his lack of crying and outward emotion.

We talked about it. It wasn't accusatory; we were simply pointing out facts. Kirk told me that sometimes he went days without thinking of Russell or feeling the pain caused by Russell's death. It later occurred to me that I could have been angry or hurt that Kirk had moved on with such apparent ease. I could have misinterpreted his lack of emotion as a lack of caring or lack of sadness. Fortunately, I didn't.

Even before Russell's death, I understood that because of Kirk's busy schedule, he could sometimes go days without thinking about *any* of the kids. But Russell was constantly at the forefront of my mind because he'd been at the forefront of my days. I accepted the way Kirk was working through his grief, and he accepted the way I was working through mine.

Kirk could have seen my lack of control as silly or overindulgent. He could have chided me, but he never did. He could have berated me for my tears, but he didn't. He could have misinterpreted my desolation as a lack of faith or disbelief in God's eternal plan, but he trusted in my testimony. He could have tried to "fix" me with his intellect, but he didn't. It seemed Kirk sensed that my emotional pain couldn't be fixed with mere words or knowledge.

Instead of trying to change me, Kirk let my emotions ebb and flow, allowing the waves of grief to crash when they came. It must have been hard for him to see a hurt he couldn't fix, to watch my pain overflow at times and not be able to help contain it. To his credit, he never tried. Kirk just loved me without restraint. He accepted me no matter where my grief took me. He never said I should cry less. And I never said he should cry more. Even though we grieved differently and separately, our grief itself connected us as a family and as a couple.

At one point, I wanted to write Russell's biography. I wanted to consolidate all the memories and thoughts and feelings interfering with my brain's ability to function. They needed a place to go because as things were, I couldn't focus on anything else but Russell. I was afraid to not think about him. I was afraid that if I let them, the memories would quietly slip away into nothingness, that they would be gone for the rest of my mortality. That idea struck me with horror, so I clung to these memories until I could give them a new place to stay.

* * *

As part of my grieving, I started writing my Russell book sometime before the first anniversary of his death. Remembering and writing were healing for me. I tried to involve the family with the project, to involve Kirk, but no one else wanted to help. It was not until I had finished the rough draft and was reading it to the children that more of their own memories resurfaced.

Then they often asked, "Did you put this in the Russell Book?"

I added their memories to mine, and then the book was truly complete. It calmed me to see that our memories of Russell were now safe. We could visit them anytime we wanted. Each time I revisited the special times in Russell's life, my troubled soul was soothed. I was also able to see more clearly how the Lord's hand had been guiding our lives. I realized that mundane experiences I'd had with Russell were really moments I was saying good-bye without knowing it. I saw how our actions, even when we didn't realize we were following the subtle promptings of the Holy Ghost—and sometimes *especially* when we didn't realize we were following His subtle promptings—were preparing us to continue living after Russell had died.

Many times as I wrote his biography, I felt Russell with me, reminding me of our fun experiences together. When I laughed at funny memories, I felt him smiling. When I cried over poignant memories, I felt him crying too. Writing Russell's story helped me loosen the chokehold I had on him. Gradually, I was able to loosen my grasp on what I knew couldn't hold. The book helped me move forward unfettered, with Russell at my side instead of me clinging to him.

Instinctively, I realized this would be *my* road to healing, not Kirk's. I was not upset that he never found time to help with the book. Kirk had a few specific memories of Russell that I needed, and he wrote those parts for me, but otherwise it was my project. My outlet. And I was fine with that.

Kirk had his own project and outlet for grief. Russell was named after Kirk's paternal grandfather. As a boy, Kirk spent many summer months and holidays with his father's side of the family, playing with his cousins, aunts, and uncles in the wild farmlands of Idaho. Kirk has many fond memories of these times as a child with his grandparents. Time spent with them was a city boy's dream vacation—they fished at the Ryrie Dam, tubed down the Snake River, shot guns, rode horses, milked cows, dug irrigation ditches, stacked wood, and hung out at Rick's College. Kirk loved camping and hiking in Yellowstone, fishing in Island Park, camping in Jackson Hole, and sightseeing in the Grand Tetons.

Unbeknownst to me, Kirk had plans to continue these traditions with our family. We had visited Idaho when Karissa and Kyle were young, but Kirk had been waiting until Russell was older for us to go back so Kirk could show Russell the stomping grounds of his namesake. Kirk looked forward to bringing Russell and the rest of the children to Idaho to experience the joy and awakening he had experienced as a child. He wanted to share the adventure with us and hoped we would form lasting bonds with extended family and come to love the land that was so dear to him.

After Russell's death, Kirk spent time reflecting on this particular loss. It was a loss of all the anticipated experiences he'd planned on sharing with Russell. Kirk thought more keenly about the time he'd spent with his cousins and realized that it had been too long since he'd seen them. They'd spent every summer together as children, but years had passed since the last time he'd talked with any of them. After Russell's death, Kirk felt a strong need to reconnect with his cousins, aunts, and uncles. He wanted to connect our family with theirs and strengthen the bond he'd once had, so he began planning a family reunion, which he aptly called the "Russell Hess Family Reunion," named after his grandfather, the patriarch of the family.

Kirk worked hard at planning the reunion. It took months of work—finding a suitable location, sending invitations and following up, planning activities and meals. He often asked me for help and tried to bounce ideas off of me. I listened, sometimes feigning interest, but was never really helpful. I was so absorbed in the Russell book that I couldn't see why the reunion was such a big deal to Kirk. I didn't understand until later how important it was to him. I hadn't met many of the people coming, so while I was looking forward to the reunion, I was not emotionally tied to it like Kirk was.

The reunion for Kirk was what the Russell book was for me. Kirk instinctively realized that he'd be completing the project without much help from his spouse, and I assume he was okay with that; we never talked about it. I wonder if he even wondered about my interest or if he was like me—so absorbed in its completion that he didn't seem to notice I wasn't there.

At the reunion, I learned more about Kirk's grieving than I had all the previous months we had lived without Russell. Kirk shared his dreams of introducing Russell to Idaho and of bringing our families together. He told of the pull he felt to reconnect with everyone, of the acute loss he felt since Russell wasn't here. Kirk opened himself up to the extended family and let everyone have a look inside. I was touched at what I saw—and was suddenly sorry I had been so caught up in my own sadness that I hadn't really bothered to look at his. But through the reunion, Kirk was able to share with me tender insights he'd gleaned throughout the experience. I'd had no idea how incredible and necessary the Russell Hess Family Reunion would be for our family.

I'd had no vision of the finished product and what good it would produce. But Kirk had. I am grateful he so willingly took on that heavy responsibility and completed it without me.

Likewise, I had the finished product of the Russell book in my head the whole time I was writing it. I knew how powerful it would be for our family and how necessary it was for me. Through the Russell book, I was able to open up in a way I was unable to verbally. I couldn't *talk* about the accident or my raw feelings, but I could *write* about them. Through the written word, my family would know how deep my testimony ran, that even though I cried all of the time, I still had faith in my Heavenly Father and knew that this was part of His plan. I needed it in writing, for all to see, because I was afraid that my overt desolation at missing Russell might confuse others and cause them to think that I was desolate in my trust of God.

Kirk and I had no idea how profoundly our individual outlets would affect each other and our families. I dare say that both the reunion and the book reconnected our immediate family as well as our extended families in ways we couldn't have imagined. I don't think that these two separate projects would have been as effective had we completed them together, nor do I think the healing process for either of us would have been as effective. Kirk and I needed to be immersed—absorbed completely, and utterly alone—in our own tasks. We needed the quiet reflection that came to us individually. And because we seemed to understand this without question, the pondering allowed our spirits to connect and be healed by the great Healer Himself.

So when I took my child to the doctor and the nurse implied that at least Kirk and I could "grieve together," I felt she misunderstood. We weren't grieving together; we were grieving side by side. It sounds terribly lonely, and at times, it really is. But grief, by its nature, is a lonely journey. I found I needed the tears that wouldn't stop coming. I needed to accept my lack of control over everything in my life and eventually embrace it. I couldn't go through that process with another person—not even my husband, who was slogging through his own grieving process.

I don't begrudge Kirk for needing to grieve differently than I did. I'm just grateful he was as accepting of my grief as I was of his. I can see how this type of intense pain can pull couples apart and cause them to withdraw in anger or hurt. It can cause rifts in a marriage that can be hard to heal.

Although we grieved differently and separately, our marriage became stronger during this intense period of pain. We weren't clinging together as I had imagined we would. Instead, strength came in the unconditional acceptance of how each of us chose to heal. It was in allowing one another space. It was our decision to love each other no matter where the grief took us individually.

In that sense, no matter how physically or emotionally far apart our grief took us, we were so entwined at the heart that we were, in a way, able to grieve together.

# Chapter Five
## MORE PRECIOUS THAN GOLD

A FEW WEEKS AFTER RUSSELL died, my good friend Stacy delivered her stillborn baby, born months too soon. The fact that she already had three children did not soften the pain of losing her baby. Together, we mourned the loss of both of our children. Sadly, while I had received a lot of support and help, my friend felt very alone. Not many people acknowledged her loss as real and valid. Some had not known she was pregnant. Others didn't realize how painful it is to lose a child whom one has never physically met. Still others simply didn't acknowledge the fetus as a child and therefore didn't feel she had lost anything. It took great effort for Stacy to look past well-meant but offensive comments like, "Just be grateful for the children you have," or, "It's not like it was a *real* baby."

As she wrestled with the grief of losing a child and the hormonal changes that seemed to pillage her emotions, she also struggled with the questions "Why this?" and "Why now?" The hardest part for Stacy was that this pregnancy was different from all her others. Prior to this pregnancy, she and her husband just seemed to *know* when it was time to add another child to their family and followed those promptings accordingly. After her third child, however, she and her husband were not sure if they should have more. They went back and forth about it for years. Earnest prayer had produced no concrete answer, so they determined it was up to them to decide. It always seemed that when she was ready, he was not and that when he was ready, she was not.

They were at a standstill when, during a quiet moment, Stacy had an unmistakable, strong spiritual witness that now was the time. She quickly became pregnant and felt that this baby really wanted to join her family.

And then she lost the baby.

So why this? And why now? Stacy had no answers. Why would she have had such a strong spiritual impression to have a baby only to lose the child?

Stacy felt that she was being punished, but for what? Stacy had been a devoted member her whole life, doing all the right things. Even as an adolescent, when many teenagers and young adults experimented and dabbled in the forbidden, she'd remained true to her beliefs. She'd married a returned missionary in the temple, and they did their best to have a Christ-centered home. She didn't deserve this. She went back and forth between anger and helplessness, between desolation and indignation. She found herself reevaluating everything from her testimony in the Church to her belief in God. She was having a trial of her faith, and she honestly didn't know what the outcome would be.

The same people who minimized Stacy's loss also questioned the struggle she was having with her faith. Surely, they thought, if she would pray more or have more faith, she'd be okay. Why wasn't she coming to church now, in her time of greatest need? Why was it taking her so long to get over it? Stacy felt unfairly judged, and that alienated her from church even more.

Then someone laid the worst judgment she felt possible on her when they told her, "You are acting like one of your children has died."

One of her children *had* died. As we grieved together, we discussed all the conflicting emotions we both faced. I realized my grief was different from hers. While we both had experienced a sudden loss, I had been given an experience at the hospital that helped me accept it. As she went through her trial of faith, questioning everything she knew, it caused me to contemplate what made our grieving so different. I came to realize that earlier in life, I had been through similar trials of my faith and had asked similar questions, which changed the way I perceived my greatest trial and, in effect, the way I perceived my Father in Heaven.

I was specifically reminded of two distinct experiences. The first occurred years ago during my mission in Denmark. The second came the day Kirk was called to be the bishop of our ward.

Missionary work in Denmark was slow for any religion. Many Danes feel a person is a religious fanatic if they go to church more than the obligatory Christmas and Easter Masses. Members of the Church are perceived to be a crazy bunch indeed. Not only do we attend a three-hour block *every* Sunday, but we also attend weekday meetings and get together occasionally on weekends and holidays—just for fun!

Being a missionary in Denmark was challenging. At times it was painful. We received daily rejection, and yet we continued to go out, day after day, looking for those searching for the truth.

I was amazed at the caliber of the members of the Church in Denmark. They were willing to be mocked, to be persecuted, and to lose friends and family for their beliefs. They banded together and strengthened each other. They brought their children up in righteousness. I learned from the strong and stalwart members of the Church in Denmark that living the gospel doesn't exempt one from pain and suffering. I saw firsthand some of their suffering, and it caused *me* pain. I also learned that God succors those who suffer for His name. Although many of the Saints I worked with were going through hard times, they tried not to complain. They were still able to see the goodness in their lives. Their faith was not diminished, and often it was strengthened during hard times.

I began to wonder why I'd been sent to Denmark—what could I possibly do or say that would improve their lives? The members seemed to do fine without me. What need did they have for an inexperienced, twenty-one-year-old American?

My mission president and his assistants were trying to help the missionaries improve our work habits and increase our faith. "How's your faith?" was a catchphrase that ran through the mission as a result of a zone conference of the same name where the mission leaders implied that as our faith increased, so would baptisms. We were challenged at another zone conference to prayerfully pick a ward family and a date and then tell that family in the name of Jesus Christ that by that date we would have a family to teach in their home. Their job was to pray for us and to pray to help us find a family. Our mission leaders promised us that if we did this, we would have a family to teach by that date.

During that conference, a date came into my mind, and I knew that we would have a baptism by that time. At the end of the meeting, I was asked to bear my testimony. As I spoke, I promised the other missionaries that my companion and I would have a baptism by that date. As impossible as it sounded, I felt it. I knew it.

My companion and I worked hard to achieve our goal. We got up extra early, skipped lunch—and sometimes dinner—to find extra time to work. We spoke to everyone we came in contact with. It was in January, one of the most miserable months of the year in Denmark. The sun rose around eight or nine and set between three and four in the afternoon. It was cold, snowy, dark, and wet. We rode bikes and sloshed around on foot throughout our entire area. We fasted; we prayed. We tried every possible way to find people to teach.

Despite all our efforts, we found only a handful of people who were even mildly interested in hearing our message—and none willing to have the full set of discussions. Some said to come back in a few months, but that was after our goal! We dutifully wrote down their addresses, sad that they weren't going to be *the one* baptized by our date.

After a few weeks of rejection, I grew jaded. Why weren't we finding anyone to baptize? Why had I felt so strongly about this random date if nothing was going to happen?

How *was* my faith?

Was this lack of investigators somehow my fault? Had I not taught with the Spirit during the few discussions we had taught? Had I not prayed enough? Had I not allowed the Lord to inspire me as to where we should go? As the date approached, I was severely tempted to sleep in or take a day off so I could blame myself if we didn't meet our goal. As it was, my companion and I had prayed more earnestly, worked harder than was required, and given more of ourselves than we ever had. I was afraid of what would happen to the little faith I had left if we didn't meet our goal.

I figured there were three possible reasons for our lack of success, and they all scared me. One: I wasn't working hard enough. Two: God had lied to me through the Holy Ghost. Or three: I had misinterpreted my feelings and answers from the Holy Ghost.

I knew it couldn't be one or two, but if it were number three, I was in real trouble. If I had misinterpreted my feelings and answers from the Holy Ghost, I had to reevaluate my entire mission—and my entire life. The problem was, I *knew* that I had felt the promptings of the Spirit. I couldn't deny my testimony of the restored Church of Jesus Christ. I had a knowledge that far surpassed my faith, but I had no answers for this predicament. The heavens seemed sealed to me as I prayed, leaving me feeling lost and alone. My own answers were not satisfying, and they created only more confusion. I only knew that I had to continue on, working as hard as I could.

During this time, a version of Christopher Logue's poem "Come to the Edge" spoke to me:

"Come to the edge," He said.

"No—I'll fall."

"Come to the edge," He said.

"No—I'll fall."

"COME TO THE EDGE!" He said.

So I came to the edge and He pushed me.

And I flew.[5]

I felt like I was being pushed off the edge of my faith. Unfortunately, I wasn't flying; I was flailing in the air and plummeting to the ground. My companion and I continued trying every possible way of finding people. Out of desperation we even tried the pray-for-the-right-area-to-tract-in approach. The idea was to study a map of our area before praying first alone and then together for guidance as to which section we should tract next. Once we felt inspired about the same section, we would continue praying, narrowing the scope, until we felt inspired about a specific street or neighborhood.

This missionary tactic had always sounded a little hokey to me, but by this point I was willing to try anything. So we prayed. But we felt no strong direction. We prayed again and again. Still nothing. I felt a small twinge about a certain section, so we chose it and prayed on, trying to find that magical street where surely one lonely soul was waiting for the truth. We finally were satisfied about the street we should work on, so we said a prayer of thanks and quickly rode our bikes there.

Our "magical street" was an empty parking lot.

We waited around, but no one showed up. Disillusioned and depressed, we went to the first street we could find with houses. We knocked doors all afternoon with no success. By the end of that day, my spirit was ragged. I felt like giving up. Our goal date was fast approaching, and we had nothing to show for it.

The worst part of all this was that up to this point, I had loved my mission. I may not have had much tangible success, but I'd been happy. I'd felt I was doing my best. I had seen lives change and improve through the miracle of Christ's Atonement, including my own. Now I was stressed out and overcome with sadness. I felt like a failure. I felt alone and bereft. And I did not know how to fix it.

It was a crucial turning point in my mission. I could see two roads ahead of me. I saw the path of the jaded missionary: giving up, not working to her potential, not having the experiences she desired, and being able to rationalize away any meaningful spiritual experiences. If she stayed in the mission field, her mission would hold little meaning. She would look back on it with little emotion and maybe even with disgust. She would hold back her gift and her potential in the future. She would not trust God or herself. It seemed like a bleak road.

The other path—one of faith—was the one I wanted to be on. But how to cross the chasm that divided me from what I expected—from that prompting of a baptism by a certain date—and what I actually got? I had to reconcile my disappointment and disillusionment with my Heavenly

Father. I had to understand why there was such a divide between the two. The problem was, I *had* prayed about it. I *had* tried to find out, but I had received no answer.

Now the question was, where would I go with the little information I had?

As I studied the scriptures, I read of people who had questioned as I now questioned—people far more deserving than I was, people far more diligent and worthy. Joseph Smith's plea in Liberty Jail became much more poignant and meaningful to me now. He had consecrated his life to God. He had sacrificed almost everything, as had many of the Saints at that time. Yet there he was, in jail and unable to help those counting on him. It wasn't just for his sake he was asking—it was for the sake of all those who looked to him for spiritual guidance. Why were the heavens closed? Where was the promised hand of the Lord to right the wrongs the Saints were facing? Why was Joseph Smith allowed to feel so alone?

I felt that I, in a small way, was there in that dark, dank, and cramped jail cell with Joseph. I knew the power of God; I had experienced it. I'd had an expectation according to the whisperings of the Spirit. So why hadn't the Lord given me what I felt He had promised?

The answer came quietly. I was flooded with a sweet outpouring of the Spirit. I was filled with an awareness of my Heavenly Father's love for me, an awareness that engulfed my soul. The sensation was so overflowing, so powerful and unexpected, that I thought I would burst. Heavenly Father knew me and knew my trials. He knew how hard I was working, and He was pleased with my work. He was pleased with *me*. I no longer felt alone. I was assured that He had been with me, watching over me throughout this trial. Even though I hadn't felt Him near, I became immersed in the knowledge that my Heavenly Father was mindful of me and what I was doing. And while He didn't give me an answer to why we hadn't found a person to baptize by our date, it didn't matter anymore. What mattered was what I'd learned through this trial.

I grew more than I had ever grown before. Our hard work was not lost on the mission. Many missionaries told us later that they'd turned up the fire too and worked harder as a result of our example. In the months that followed the infamous date—which passed without a baptism—my companion and I taught more than we had ever taught before. We went back to all of those people who had told us to come back later. We saw lives change. We saw people grow. We saw burdens lifted. We even saw some of these people eventually enter the waters of baptism.

In the end, I still don't know why I received such an undeniable prompting about that date. I have to accept that I don't have a satisfactory answer to why it didn't happen the way I'd expected. But I came to realize that I didn't really *need* an answer to the why, no matter how badly I would like one. All I know is that I did the Lord's work to the best of my ability and that He was pleased with it.

I didn't realize that there would be many more times that the why of a situation would go unanswered. Even when I have done all that I can do, there are still times when I don't know why things have to be a certain way. The only answer I get is the one I received on my mission: my Heavenly Father loves me. And I am starting to realize that, at times, that answer is enough.

I became a new person because of this trial. I had to decide which path I would take. I was forced to spend more time on my knees, really talking to the Lord, and that gave me a new perspective. As I was stretched, I became a more understanding individual. I saw people as children of a loving Heavenly Father, and I was more sympathetic to their trials. I became a more effective missionary and was better able to reach the sad, the lonely, and the helpless. I now knew who to look for and what to say because I could, on some level, relate to how they felt.

I knew with a surety that these experiences were for my good. I had stumbled and fallen. I felt alone and afraid for a while, but when I looked up, I felt hands reaching down to help me, brushing me off and carrying me until I was strong enough to stand. Those hands held mine as we traveled down the road. I recognized those hands; the nail prints in them reminded me that He had suffered loneliness and fear far worse than mine. He knew how I felt, and I could trust that He would always be there for me.

Because of the relationship that was forged in a cold, dark moment in a Danish town so many years ago, I could see the Lord's hand even as Russell was taken home. I still don't understand why he had to leave me so soon. In the days after his death, I did not know how I would survive the pain that felt like a knife stabbing at my heart. I did not know how to break out of the fog that seemed to engulf me, but I knew that my Savior would not leave me. I had tried His love and found it to be true. No matter how lonely and disheartened I became or would become, this time I never felt alone. My all-wise, all-knowing, all-loving Heavenly Father knew who I was. He knew what I was suffering. He knew what I was feeling. And He was there to succor me and to help me live with these indescribably painful emotions for as long as they would rip at my very heartstrings. Of this I have no doubt.

As Stacy and I mourned our losses together, I realized that my mission experience had prepared me for what was to come. And I realized that God, in His wisdom, had taught me a companion lesson even more recently, a lesson that reinforced my knowledge of His awareness of each of us and our needs.

The year before Russell died, our stake was being realigned, and we knew our ward would be affected. We all drew our imaginary lines of how the ward might be split. I was worried, not for me—although I did not look forward to being separated from some of my ward friends—but for Karissa. She was the only active girl in her Primary class and had been for quite a long time. This had been hard on her, especially since she was the only girl in our family.

Karissa did have a few really good friends in the ward, but they were in the Primary class above her, so she couldn't interact with them all of the time. We worried how the ward realignment would affect her. What if her friends were split from the ward? There didn't seem to be any good answer to our worries. Our only option was to take this problem to the Lord and lay it at His feet.

This may have seemed like a small thing, but Karissa was starting to dislike coming to church because of it. She felt uncomfortable in a class full of rowdy boys. Karissa was at a critical stage. She was just starting to recognize the Holy Ghost's influence in her life, the seeds of her testimony just starting to take root. Yet here she was, struggling to go to church. I know there is more to church attendance than the social aspect, but Karissa didn't quite get that yet. I know far too many instances of people who, as kids, never felt comfortable at church and because of that are not very active as adults.

At church Karissa felt lonely, left out. That was the wrong environment for her testimony to grow in. I wanted a girl her age to move into the ward, someone who would help make church an inviting place for Karissa to attend.

I pondered and contemplated the ward split again and again, brooding over what would happen to my daughter as a result. Karissa and I discussed the possibilities, along with the best ways to handle them. Sick with fear and apprehension, I tried to prepare her for the worst. In my quiet moments—not that I had many with a new baby in tow—I found myself begging, pleading with the Lord to have mercy on my daughter and to make this transition a good one for her.

A week before the split, I found myself alone in the car, something that hadn't happened since before Joey was born nine months previous. No kids, no babies, no noise. Just me and Heavenly Father. I was about to begin my usual pleadings when I was overcome with the sweetest, most loving sensation. I was filled with joy, peace, calm. I realized that Karissa was also Heavenly Father's child and that He loved her even more than I could.

It was a concept I hadn't even considered. I was so busy asking and nagging and begging that I hadn't taken the time to listen. I had been like a child who assumed the answer was no and then did everything in her power to change it. I had been relentless—and I know how annoying that is because I have five children and have been under assault many times! Nevertheless, my Heavenly Father was patient with me. I don't know how many times He had already tried to answer my pleadings; I simply couldn't hear His quiet words above the sound of my cries. In that quiet moment, however, I did more than hear. I experienced His overwhelming love and concern for my daughter, for His daughter. I felt He was watching over her and would help her, whether that meant she lost all of her friends in the ward or that she gained new ones. His Hand was guiding our lives, and if I stopped shouting at Him long enough to look for His guidance, I would be able to see that.

I gained a new perspective that day, one that changed my relationship with my Heavenly Father a second time. I didn't receive an answer to the question I had asked, that of giving Karissa friends at church. Instead, I felt His engulfing love for my children—not just me—and I knew that He cared for them as much as He cared for me.

When Russell died almost exactly a year later, I didn't worry about him being alone or scared in his new surroundings. I didn't feel that Russell had been snatched by a vengeful God who'd taken him away to punish me for some random misdeed. Nor did I feel that Russell returned home to a God who'd been too busy with other things to see the potential danger of Russell's sled ride. I felt that Russell had returned home to a loving, deeply caring, emotionally involved Father who knew it was time for Russell to come home.

This God, the Heavenly Father I have come to know and worship, loves my children fiercely. He knows them and loves them with a compassion so vast I cannot even begin to experience or understand it. I have felt just a small portion of that love and compassion, and I know this is how Heavenly Father feels about *all* of His children. We are dear and precious to Him. He is devoted to our eternal well-being, even when that sometimes seems to conflict with our earthly well-being.

I have had challenging experiences where I did not feel a closeness to my Heavenly Father. These experiences tried my testimony and my resolve to live the gospel. But I do not feel that Russell or my family were abandoned when Russell died. I did not feel forsaken by my Heavenly Father after Russell's death. Ever.

That day in the car, I experienced the emotionally overpowering sensation of His love as I received an answer to my prayer for Karissa. I experienced this same outpouring of love again in the emergency room where I said my earthly good-byes to Russell. I realized then that His love would not shield us from the experiences we need in order to grow and progress toward becoming like Him. His love instead gives us the power to endure these experiences.

That day in my car, I put Karissa in my Heavenly Father's hands. I put my family there too, telling Him of my trust and reliance on His will, whatever that might be. I felt light; all of the burdens that had been weighing upon my soul were mercifully lifted. I had no more answers to the boundary change than I did before, but because I'd felt the magnitude of my Heavenly Father's love and the overpowering strength of that love, the details did not matter. As long as I was on the Lord's side, it would all work out the way it needed to.

Later that same night, the blessings of my decision to put my family in the Lord's hands became even clearer. We received a phone call from the stake president's secretary, and shortly thereafter, Kirk was called to be the bishop of our soon-to-be realigned ward. Despite being a busy young mother of five, I knew this was the right call for my husband and our family. A day earlier, I might have felt overwhelmed at the prospect of the call, but because of my experience that day I felt only peace.

In both of these experiences, my prayers were answered—not in the way I expected, but in the way I needed.

* * *

It's hard in the moment to understand why we're given specific trials. Often, but not always, the reason becomes clear with time. And as much as I found comfort in having someone to cry with in Stacy, seeing her suffer over the death of the child in her womb was heart wrenching for me. Still, thanks to the trials my Heavenly Father allowed me to experience, her wrestlings reminded me of my own. It made me grateful that I'd been prepared for the loss of my son. It strengthened my relationship with my Heavenly Father and helped me to better understand His nature—to see Him as a real, present, loving Being and not just as some intangible idea in my head.

As I watched my dear friend's struggles, I knew she would get through this. She was questioning all she knew, but she was looking for the answers in the right places. I knew they would come for her as they had come for me. I also knew they would not come easily. One has to be willing to work to get answers to soul-wrenching questions. I was grateful that Stacy, though she was hurting, was willing to work through the pain to find answers.

Around this time, Kirk received a call and had to leave unexpectedly. As bishop, he was occasionally called away for member emergencies. Usually I was okay with this, but on this particular day I had been looking forward to having Kirk at home. When he left, I felt incredibly sad and empty. I needed my husband, but he was off taking care of someone else.

*What about me?* I thought. *I need him too!*

I was angry and acting a little selfish. Okay, maybe a lot selfish. I wanted him to focus on my needs.

Quietly, softly, the thought came into my mind, *What if Kirk is visiting Stacy?*

He might have been. I don't know who he visited that night.

*What if her need is great tonight? Would you share him with her?*

If she was in need and Kirk could help, I would not only *not* begrudge his time away, but I would also welcome it. I realized that I had many friends in the ward but didn't know even a fraction of their worries or problems. They'd been so generous with my family; how could I be angry or selfish if Kirk had gone to help any of them? I couldn't. My anger melted away. Again I was happy to be married to a man who was so faithful and righteous that the Lord entrusted him with the souls of His children.

Many times since that night, I have pondered the experiences I have been given that have helped prepare me, strengthen me, and give me the tools necessary for living through the excruciating pain of sudden loss.

The purpose of this life is for us to prepare ourselves to meet God. It is not designed to be easy or carefree. It is designed to give us experiences that try our faith and force us to face our fears. These experiences try our patience and our endurance to help us see what we are made of and how hard we are willing to work. These trials are blessings in disguise. They aren't pleasant or even desired, but they are valuable.

Peter, that faithful "fisher of men," wrote about our life experiences in these words: "That the trial of your faith, being much more precious than of gold that perisheth, though it be tried with fire, might be found unto praise and honour and glory at the appearing of Jesus Christ."[6]

Stacy, who eventually got the answers she was searching for, has become a much stronger person because of the trial of her faith. I too have grown and stretched and learned as a result of the trials and hardships I have been asked to endure. And like Peter, I have found each of these experiences to be more precious to me than gold.

## Chapter Six

### ISOLATION

ALTHOUGH I KNEW MY HEAVENLY Father was never far, it wasn't the same when it came to my relationships with those of this earth existence. I felt so alone in my grief and my pain. My friends could not understand it, although they tried to. I tried explaining how devastatingly sad I felt all the time. How physically, emotionally, and spiritually tired I was all the time. My body hurt. My brain hurt. My heart hurt. And my soul began to hurt because I felt so alone. No one I knew or spent time with on a regular basis could *really* understand the changes forcing themselves on me the first year after Russell died.

Losing a child is an isolating event on so many levels. It ripped me away from my comfortable, normal life and threw me into a scary, lonely place. I could see my friends on the outside, living in their innocence and enjoying the sun. We could talk, but they could not come into the darkness engulfing me. It was as if there was an abyss they could not bridge. With suffocating sadness, I realized I'd never be returning to that happy and simple state. And no one could join me.

I began reading books by people who'd lost children. I talked to newfound friends who'd lost children. And I didn't feel so alone; I'd found others who truly understood my pain. While I was sad that they understood my pain only because they had also lost a child, I was grateful for the company. I felt less crazy because we shared similar experiences, emotions, situations. It surprised me how much I had in common with total strangers, just through our similar losses.

A peculiar thing we all seemed to share was the borderline offensive comments from people who didn't know what to say: "At least you have other children," or "You can always have another," as if the life of a child could be so easily replaced and forgotten. Such comments were usually made by well-meaning individuals who simply didn't know what else to say and felt that they must say *something*.

What disturbed me was the reaction my new friends often had to these insulting comments. They said things like, "You really find out who your *real* friends are," and, "After *that* comment, I never talked to them again."

That made me sad. Losing a child is isolating enough without isolating ourselves even more because someone has said the wrong thing in ignorance. I realized the motive behind the hurtful comments wasn't to hurt but to help in some way, awkward as that might be.

I learned this lesson earlier in a very personal, agonizing way.

Our neighbors to the right had two older school-aged kids. Our neighbors to the left had one older daughter and one Karissa's age. We couldn't believe our luck! We became great friends as we sat outside watching the girls play. Our neighbor on the right got pregnant that first year, and the other neighbor and I both got pregnant a few months later. We all were expecting boys and spent much time planning how fun our futures would be with our sons running around.

Then my neighbor to the left received disturbing news. An ultrasound showed that her baby had a severe heart defect. The doctors warned that her baby would need at least three major heart surgeries within the first six months of life—the first to be performed immediately after birth. By the time he was sixteen—if he lived that long—he would need a heart transplant. At the devastating news, we mourned for our neighbor and the loss of the future we had all planned. Aside from the major heart defect, it was determined that my neighbor's baby was otherwise healthy. And so, although she anticipated years of health struggles with this child, this neighbor also looked forward to many happy memories.

A healthy, happy child was born to my neighbor on the right. He was about four months old when my son Kyle was born. When Kyle was twenty days old, my neighbor's husband came over to share heartbreaking news. With no warning or explanation, their vibrant, lively baby had died of sudden infant death syndrome. He'd simply stopped breathing while taking a nap.

The news rocked our little neighborhood. This kind of thing just didn't happen to people we knew! What to do? I felt like I had to do *something*, but I had no idea what. Here I had a tiny baby of my own. I couldn't just knock on my neighbor's door, Kyle in tow, and ask how she was doing. I felt a deep sense of my own inadequacy. I desperately wanted to make things better, but I just couldn't. I had no idea what to say or how to say it.

I'm sure I said stupid things. I hope whatever I said wasn't hurtful.

A week later the other neighbor's baby was born. While they had braced themselves for a child with a serious heart problem, they had no idea he'd also been afflicted with a rare neurological condition that affected his whole body, not just his heart. Instead of being whisked away into immediate heart surgery as planned, he was put on a respirator. The parents were told he wouldn't live on his own. They were given a few days to prepare before they would need to turn off the respirator.

This again was shocking news for the neighborhood. We prayed that a miracle might occur when the respirator was turned off. But the miracle we asked for didn't come.

This was January 1999. A gloom set over the entire neighborhood as we mourned over the losses of our neighbors. Where normally I felt confident and able to answer life's questions, I now felt inept. My condolences seemed clumsy, my speech bungled as I tried to hold a conversation with my dear, suffering friends. I didn't want to say the wrong thing, and that fear paralyzed me into saying nothing at all. I was afraid to see my neighbors when I went outside—afraid that I would hurt them through my incompetence.

Sometimes I avoided them when they were outside. I wanted so desperately to talk to them, to let them know how sorry I was for their pain, but I couldn't express my feelings. I was so sad for my neighbors, but I didn't want to cry in front of them, to make them cry, to make things worse. When I did talk to them, I'm sure I avoided mentioning their loss. I'm sure I brought up God and heaven and eternal life, as if the mere mention of these things could somehow take away their staggering pain. I wanted to share what I knew of eternal families. But sharing the promise of something so happy just seemed wrong at a time like that. My neighbors were polite, even nice to me, but I know my efforts were lacking.

A few days after the second baby died, the parents who'd lost their baby to SIDS walked over to my other neighbor's house. They made a sad procession, walking slowly, hand in hand, to offer words of comfort to another family suffering the same loss. I watched them from my window, my heart breaking again.

*What are they saying to each other?* I wondered. *What kind of consolation are they giving?* I assumed that they knew exactly what to say. That they had all the answers. That somehow their conversation would be easier than talking with them had been for me simply because they were in the same situation.

When Russell died, we were in the same house with these same neighbors on either side. This same couple visited us, as I knew they would. When I saw them walking slowly up our walk, I waited to hear their sage advice. But they had no words to offer other than, "We are sorry for your loss because we know how painful it is."

*They have no answers.* They had no pointers on how to navigate the storm. But they had tears, and they shed them openly. They had the courage to talk to us.

Later, when other friends tried to comfort *me* with platitudes, I remembered my feelings of inadequacy in being able to "fix things" for my friends. I remembered the anxiety that caused me to avoid them. I remembered the foolish things I said because I thought they were comforting. I remembered these things because I was now the recipient of the downcast eyes that wouldn't meet mine, the friends who would talk about anything else except Russell, the friends who offered words of comfort like, "At least you have other kids," and "At least we know what we know," thinking that by speaking they were filling the uncomfortable silence with something that would help.

Some friends wouldn't even talk to me anymore—and I knew why they couldn't: it was too scary and painful. I understood. I could truly empathize with them. My experience with my neighbors' babies taught me that. That experience gave me compassion for my well-meaning friends. I recognized the intent behind their careless-sounding remarks, the fear and concern behind the evasions.

A chasm now stood between me and those who had never suffered great loss, and I realized that *I* would have to bridge that gap to maintain the relationship. If I did not make the first step toward them, they would eventually retreat from the edge of their side of the bridge, never to talk normally again to me. I was a little grumpy about having to take that first step, to say hello and talk to them, but then I remembered my own paralyzing fear. I still have so many regrets about the way I handled the deaths of my neighbors' children. I didn't want any of my friends to have the same regrets years from now. I did not want our friendships to become stunted or wither away.

I'm still sad for the losses my neighbors incurred that bleak January so many years ago. And I wish I could have been different. Instead, I was naive and timid. But I'm grateful for what I learned during that time. It made me more understanding and empathetic when Russell died. It made me less judgmental and more forgiving. It allowed me to open doors instead of sitting behind shut ones, wondering why I was still so alone. It kept me connected with people who may have been too afraid to stay in touch, empowering all of us to be united and to mourn together.

# Chapter Seven
## THE MEMORY QUILT

A FEW YEARS BEFORE RUSSELL died, a family in my ward lost their adult daughter when she was hit by a car and killed instantly as she was driving on the freeway early one Sunday morning.

The same inadequacies I'd felt with the losses of my neighbors' children washed over me. I wanted to fix the situation for this family so dear to me. I wanted to make it better or at least less painful for them. But I knew there wasn't much I could do besides share my condolences. I watched, however, and learned from what others offered them—like the woman who sang at the funeral and her accompanist. The accompanist transposed the notes of the song so that the singer could sing it, and both offered the grieving family a gift of beauty at their daughter's funeral. It was something they could look back on and remember with a smile.

Was there a gift I could give that would have the same effect?

As I wondered what I could do for the family, the idea to make a memory quilt popped in my head. I love to quilt. A lady in my ward taught a group of us the basics, and from there I took off. I found that I think in quilts. I plan more quilts than I will ever be able to make, but I *love* picking out just the right colors, cutting up the pieces, and sewing them together. I love to see my creation growing, to watch it take life. But most of all, I love to see the face of the person I give the quilt to.

When I asked the mother if she would be interested in one, she began laying aside some of the clothes her daughter wore so that I could use them for the squares. Each piece of fabric would bring back special memories for the family as they looked at it. I'd never made a quilt from clothes before, and so I began researching the best way to go about it.

Before this, I'd never gone through the grieving process with another person. Sure, I'd tried—clumsily—with my neighbors. Now I talked with my friend as we planned the quilt. She shared funny stories and memories of her daughter. We laughed and we cried during the months it took her to pick out which clothes to use. Weeks after that, we went to the fabric store together so she could choose background material that would best represent her daughter, who loved purple and butterflies and flowers. The quilt began to belong to the mother well before I cut out a single piece. She decided on an antique circle block as the outside border of the quilt. The twelve-inch blocks would be made up of her daughter's clothes. Inside the border on the top half, we sewed in a professionally embroidered poem the daughter had written. The bottom half had a paper-pieced picture of an angel on one side and one of her dog's shirts on the other.

It took me a substantial amount of time to back all the fabric, cut it, and sew it all into the antique circle blocks. Then I let the mother know I was done with the blocks and ready for her to arrange them the way she wanted. It took her a few weeks to be emotionally ready to see the squares. After she designed the arrangement, I sewed the middle part to the outside border. The quilting and binding took a few weeks more.

The twin-size quilt took more than a year to complete, and while I made it, I learned a little more about the grieving process. I learned the ups and downs—and the downs and downs—of losing a child. I learned to work on the mother's time frame, and I learned that talking about her loss wasn't scary although it was extremely sad. I felt empowered because I finally had something to offer. But even as I gave this time and talent to my friend, she gave me something more valuable: the courage to talk to the grieving.

She helped me learn what was helpful and what wasn't. She taught me that it is better to say something about the loss than to say nothing. The experience not only gave me the tools as an outsider to understand the anguish of loss, but it gave me better insight when I experienced it myself.

When I let my friend know that I was finally finished with the quilt, it took a while for her to be able to come see it. I think we both realized how monumental it was for me to pass the quilt on to her. I was sad to see it go; it had been a part of my life for so long. Again we laughed and cried together. We reminisced about her daughter and the memories we'd made together. I was honored to have been able to give the family a small token of their daughter's life.

Later, her husband complained to me that she'd put the quilt under her bed instead of leaving it out. He knew how much time had been spent making the quilt and felt that it should be displayed. His wife got it out only when she needed to feel close to her daughter. And when the pain grew too intense, she gently folded it and put it out of sight. I completely understood.

Well, I didn't completely understand then. I did later, when I lost Russell and I made a quilt for him. But back when I first made the quilt, I understood my friend's need to put the quilt away, at least on some level. I'd made it for her to use however it would best meet her needs.

A week or two before I passed the quilt on, another friend asked if I would be interested in making another memory quilt. A friend of hers had lost a son five years before and was now ready to do something with his clothes. Since I still had the first quilt, my friend's friend came over to see it. It was just what she'd envisioned for her son's quilt, only she wanted something more masculine looking.

I made two quilts——one for her and her husband and one for their other son. These quilts went much faster, not only because I didn't piece the clothes into antique circles but because this friend was emotionally ready.

This quilt was also a learning experience for me. Not only did I make a valuable new friend, but I also learned more about how the grieving process still affects people years after a loved one dies. Her grief was not as raw and vulnerable as the other mother's, but it was just as painful and intense. Again, I learned that I could talk to her about it and that doing so made her cry. But releasing those emotions was not the bad thing I thought it would be. I learned that the crying strengthened the connection she had with her son and that it strengthened the connection we were beginning to have.

When her quilts were done, she and her husband laid their quilt on their dead son's bed so that when they went into his room they would remember the fun times they'd had with him. The quilt is still there today. My friend says sometimes she pulls it off the bed and just wraps herself in it. She closes her eyes and tries to imagine being lost in her son's embrace.

After Russell died, I knew I would one day make a quilt in remembrance of him. But I couldn't bear to do it right away. Instead, I packed the clothes I planned to use. I closed the drawer and walked away for a while. In the meantime I made a trip quilt to commemorate the fun things we did on our last adventure with Russell. It *had* been a fun trip. I didn't want it to be the "trip Russell died on," and I thought that making a quilt would help us remember the fun family things we'd done together. Each family member did a square, drawing a picture of their favorite part of the trip. I sewed them all together with happy, bright colors. On the top, I paper-pieced

the phrase "Our Family Is Forever." On the back, I wrote the reason for
the quilt and my testimony of the plan of salvation.

When I finished the quilt, however, I couldn't bear to look at it. No
matter how I tried to dress it up, this *was* still the trip when Russell died.
It was still too tender to touch. I folded the quilt and hung it, testimony-
side out, on our stair banister. I just didn't know what to do with it. I was
a little perplexed that I didn't feel any better after making the quilt.

I *was* happy it was done. I wanted to have it for documentation's sake
if nothing else. But it brought me little joy. I'm sure I cried the entire time
I worked on it.

It took me awhile before I was able to work on Russell's memory quilt.
About six months after he died, I pulled the shirts out of the drawer and
cut them in half. Then I put them away again. Another day, months later,
I ironed on the backing to stabilize the fabric. Some months after that,
I trimmed the pieces down to size. Then one day, I got them out of the
drawer and sewed the borders around each square. Eventually I sewed all
of the squares together. I took my time, doing only a little at a time for a
short period of time. Then, after a good heart-wrenching cry, I'd put the
project away for another few weeks or months until I felt I could bear to
look at Russell's clothes again.

After the middle of the quilt was done, I got my favorite pictures of
Russell printed on fabric and repeated the process of backing fabric and
sewing borders around each block. I embroidered my favorite drawings
that Russell drew and added them. Then I embroidered about eighty of
Russell's favorite sayings around the outside border. Again I used bright,
happy colors; the superhero reds, yellows, and blues of his shirts called
out to be wrapped in vibrant colors. I wanted the quilt to be a celebration
of his life, and I couldn't do that with dark, drab colors, even if those
were the colors I tended to see those days. The back of the quilt had the
Spiderman fabric my mom and her friends made the ties and hair bows
from for the funeral.

I took the quilt to my friend's long-arm quilting machine and quilted
it myself. I'm still a novice in the quilting department, so I practiced for
days before I dared put my Russell quilt in the machine. I could have paid
to have it professionally quilted, but I'm pretty cheap. Besides, I wanted
to do this myself. I wanted to make it from start to finish.

It took me a year to complete it. It might have brought me some
closure, but it didn't bring Russell back. It didn't give me the boost I was

looking for. It gave me some happy moments and brought back some happy memories, but shirts and fabric are cheap comparisons to a lively, energetic, happy child.

I didn't want a quilt—I wanted Russell.

I folded up the quilt and hung it on a quilt rack. I get it out to look at it every once in a while, but when the memories become too painful, I fold the quilt back up and put it away. Maybe when the feeling isn't as sharp and heavy, I'll be able to display it. I'm still not sure. I'm still making memory quilts for anyone who asks.

They're helpful in their own way, but I always tell the recipient that I'll understand if the quilt spends more time packed away than out.

## Chapter Eight
### SORROW

I HADN'T EXPERIENCED MUCH LOSS before Russell died and was very naive about the subject of grief. When someone died after a long, painful illness, I thought that person's family must be relieved, happy even, that their loved one was now no longer in pain. When someone righteous died too soon, I believed that the knowledge of the plan of salvation swallowed up any sadness of the death. And when children died before the age of accountability . . . how lucky those parents were. Their children had made it! I knew death brought heartache, but I also thought the heartache would melt away in the joy of the future.

Even in the emergency room when I said good-bye to Russell, amid all the sadness and heartbreak, I assumed the grieving process wouldn't be so bad. After all, I was starting at the "acceptance stage"! Didn't that mean I completely passed the stages of denial, anger, bargaining, and depression?

Alma the Younger, after wading through terrible guilt and grief over his sins, caught hold of the Atonement of Jesus Christ. He described at first being "racked with torment" and "harrowed up" in his pains. After repenting, Alma recorded that he "could remember [his] pains no more" and "oh, what joy and what marvelous light [he] did behold" for his "soul was filled with joy as exceeding as was [his] pain" (Alma 36:17–20).

When Russell died, I was living the best I could. Since I didn't have any major sins to repent of, I assumed that meant I wouldn't be harrowed up in any kind of pain, or at least a pain that would last very long. Sure I would be *sad*—I missed Russell terribly. But any day now, I would feel those pains no more and start feeling that joy Alma talked about.

But instead of feeling that joy, I continued to feel excruciatingly lost and empty. This lesson in grief was devastating. I had no idea I'd be so painfully sad, that instead of rejoicing in his passing I would wonder if I could ever be able to fully rejoice again. I'd erroneously interpreted the plan of salvation—thinking it would assuage my grief and that I would only feel peace, joy, and consolation. I think that is a common misconception, and because I expected it to be so much easier, I felt blindsided and completely unprepared for the pain I actually felt.

While slogging through this part of the grieving process, I was reminded of someone's grief I'd observed four years before. I hadn't quite understood the depth of his grief then, but suddenly it made sense.

President Hinckley was the first counselor in the First Presidency when I served my mission in Denmark. I was familiar with this happy man and had enjoyed listening to his dry wit and uplifting talks for years. When my mission president announced that President Hinckley, his wife, and some other General Authorities would be visiting Denmark and speaking to the missionaries, I was ecstatic! I was so excited to see him in person and hear his message. Sitting at a General Authority's feet, hearing his words of wisdom, would be an amazing experience. What I remember most about that whole experience, though, was not what was spoken but what I saw.

President Hinckley treated Sister Hinckley with such care and respect that his love for her radiated from his very being. They held hands. He opened doors for her and helped her up and down the stairs. He was attentive to her every need. And that's not to say she had many needs; she was just getting older. President Hinckley's thoughtful gestures spoke to me of the deep love and tenderness he felt for her. And I could see by the way Sister Hinckley reciprocated his actions that she loved him just as deeply.

In the 2003 general Relief Society meeting, President Hinckley said this about his wife:

> Now to you dear grandmothers, you older widows, and older lonely women. How beautiful you are. I look upon my dear wife, soon to be 92 years of age. Her hair is white; her frame is stooped.
>
> I take one of her hands in mine and look at it. Once it was so beautiful, the flesh firm and clear. Now it is wrinkled and a little bony and not very strong. But it speaks of love and constancy and faith, of hard work through the years. Her memory is not what it once was. She can remember things that happened half a century ago but may not remember what happened half an hour ago. I am like that, too.
>
> But I am so grateful for her. For 66 years we have walked together, hand in hand, with love and encouragement, with appreciation and respect. It cannot be very long before one of us will step through

the veil. I hope the other will follow soon. I just would not know how to get along without her, even on the other side, and I would hope that she would not know how to get along without me.[7]

I remember hearing when Sister Hinckley died on April 6, 2004, and being surprised. Even though they were both almost a century old, I never really thought either of them *could* die. I just assumed that President and Sister Hinckley would be around for my children to enjoy. I was sad for President Hinckley, but if I mourned, it was only for a short time. Back then I was still under the impression that the death of a righteous loved one wasn't such a *sad* thing. It would bring tears, of course, but since we knew where Sister Hinckley was—in the arms of loved ones and eternally saved in Jesus Christ—we should be celebrating, not mourning.

So I was filled with perplexed bewilderment as I watched President Hinckley over the next year. He still led the Church; he still visited the Saints around the world, but he seemed to have changed. He now appeared frail and weak. He seemed to have lost some of his zest for life. He'd lost something—something I could not put my finger on.

How could he be so sad? President Hinckley, of all people, knew where his wife was, but that first year he seemed so lost without her. I thought maybe he would die soon too of a broken heart. I marveled at the idea as I watched him. These observations taught me a lot. As I wondered about his grief, I learned more about mourning the death of a loved one. I slowly learned that the process lasts a long, long time. And maybe it never really goes away.

President Hinckley, in his opening comments in the April 2005 general conference, said, "We have traveled the earth bearing witness of this, the work of the Almighty. During these same years I personally have traveled nearly a million miles visiting some seventy countries. My beloved companion traveled with me until a year ago when she passed away on the 6th of April. It has been lonely since then."[8]

The next year, in the April 2006 general conference, President Hinckley said: "My beloved companion of 67 years left me two years ago. I miss her more than I can say. She was really a remarkable woman, one with whom I walked side by side in perfect companionship for more than two-thirds of a century. As I look back upon my life, I do so with a measure of wonder and awe. Everything good that has happened, including my marriage, I owe to my activity in the Church."[9]

After this talk, I noticed that President Hinckley seemed to have some of his old spunk back. He seemed to travel more, and he seemed to be much busier than he had the previous two years. He was almost like a man who had awoken from a very long sleep who had to work hard to catch up on all the work he'd missed. President Hinckley seemed to be on fire. His zeal to visit the Saints returned, and he seemed anxious to get things done. I remember being surprised that it had taken him so long and suddenly realizing that maybe the separation from a loved one caused a deeper rift than I had imagined.

\* \* \*

The day after Russell died, a couple around our age came over to talk to us. They had lost a six-year-old son two months before in an accident. Like we had, they'd experienced the comforting arm of the Lord embracing them at the hospital and throughout the next two months. They felt, like we did, that this was no accident but part of the Lord's plan for their family, that it was their son's time to go. But they were still crying. They were still so sad. I sat there, numbly listening and taking mental notes.

*In two months, I may still be crying?*

I was looking for my time frame—when would happiness and peace set in? If I would still be crying in two months, when would I *stop* crying? I really thought there would be a time I would be able to talk about Russell's death without tears.

Then the wife said something that gave me hope: "Things will never get back to normal, but you'll find a new normal."

I liked that thought. I had given birth to five kids. After each one, we'd floundered for about six months and then settled into our "new normal." Life wasn't the same as it had been before each child was born, but it was just as comfortable and happy, albeit a bit louder and more chaotic.

So I started waiting for our new normal to arrive. I'd done this before, I thought. Adjusting this time wouldn't be the same as with a new baby, but I pictured myself eventually comfortable and happy.

The day we flew home, a car service drove us to the airport after we stopped at the mortuary to pick up Russell's casket. On the way to the airport, the driver struggled to compose himself. He and I made eye contact in the rearview mirror a few times; tears welled up in his eyes and spilled down his cheeks.

*Odd that a complete stranger is so overcome at our grief,* I thought. As we got out of the car, I gave the driver a tissue. He apologized and told me that his sister had died about thirteen years before.

"It's still painful," he said.

Thirteen years later, his emotions seemed brand-new, his wound gaping. I was saddened that I didn't have any words of cheer for him. I thought I should since I was going through something similar. It was one of the first experiences that taught me that there really was nothing adequate that I could say.

Shouldn't I have the perfect, comforting remarks to bind up pain and make it better? I couldn't reconcile his raw, fresh grief with my assumption that all would be better when that blessed new normal finally arrived.

A few days before the funeral, I received a call from the Newport Beach Temple president. He'd lost a child thirty-five years before. A friend of his in our ward had told him about Russell and asked if he could call us to give us some words of encouragement. I knew a little of his story, and I was expecting his call, so I wasn't surprised to hear his voice on the other end of the line. What did surprise me, though, was his emotional state. After introducing himself, he said he'd heard about Russell. Then he stopped talking, so choked up he couldn't continue.

With the phone to my ear, I sat there, stunned. His child had passed away thirty-five years before, and he was still crying as if it had happened yesterday. How could he still be so sad?

I finished his introduction for him, telling him I'd heard about his son, and gave my condolences. We spoke briefly about heaven, the eternities, and the mercy of our Heavenly Father's plan. The conversation ended with both of us in tears. As I hung up, my brain couldn't wrap itself around the fact that this man was still grieving. He was a strong member of the Church, a member of the Seventy, a temple president! He knew the plan of salvation. He knew where his son was. And after thirty-five years, talking about his son still made him cry.

This was so far from my expectation of how death affected others. My surprise and awe slowly turned to fear. This would be worse and last even longer than I'd ever imagined.

A few weeks later, I spoke with a friend who'd lost an adult daughter three years before.

"You'll never be the same," she told me. "You'll be sad for a long, long time, and it'll never go away."

At my dismay, she tried to comfort me with, "It gets better and less raw with time, but the feeling of loss will be there until you're with Russell again."

I was aghast! This was someone I *knew*, someone I talked with regularly. And she lived with this depth of sadness every day? On the surface she seemed to be fine. If you knew her well, you could detect a hint of sadness in her eyes, but it wasn't much. I thought she'd hit her new normal and embraced life with joy. She seemed so happy and regular—not like someone in constant pain and longing.

I didn't want to hear this prediction of what my future held, but still she continued.

"You'll feel fine one day, like you're done being sad. Then out of nowhere, the pain and depression will hit again. You'll travel through grief this way for years." She said it all with such certainty and peace, but I was ready to scream. She wasn't done yet. "The waves of sadness will blindside you at times, causing you to cry in places you don't expect or want, and don't feel bad about it because you'll have no control over your reactions. You'll be able to tone them down a bit over time, but ultimately your grief will never end. The loss will never actually be filled. My heart will never again be the same."

I wanted her to stop, but like viewing a car wreck, I couldn't seem to take my eyes off of her. I couldn't stop listening to the horrific future ahead of me.

Another friend who was listening cut in. "Stop telling her such depressing things!"

The response: "I can't. Jenny needs to know the cold, hard truth. She needs to know that when she breaks down in the middle of the supermarket because of the song playing overhead, it's normal. That she's *not* going crazy because when these things happen, she's going to feel like she *is* crazy. She needs to hear—from someone who has been there—that it never ends. The pain gets less sharp, but it will always hurt."

My head was spinning. I couldn't take all of her words in at once.

As the days wore on, I still didn't think about them too much; I was too busy crying. Eventually I read books by people who had lost children. My friend's counsel was a common thread in each of their stories: they could still live, but it always hurt.

Slowly and by degrees, I saw the error of my previous thinking. It was foolishness, wishful thinking, to suppose that anyone could get through this kind of loss without irrevocable and life-altering damage. I could eventually continue on with life, but I would never move on from my son's death. My heart would always have a special spot for this experience. The memories would always hurt.

This concept hit me most fully about four months after Russell died. I was still searching for the new normal but coming to terms with the idea that I still had months of crying and debilitating sadness ahead. One day I drove the children somewhere. They were laughing and chatting, singing and teasing each other. All at once a flood of emotion washed over me. I missed Russell so profoundly and fiercely. He wasn't there in the car, jumping in the conversation and adding his two cents. He loved his siblings, and they loved him. They enjoyed being together. I ached for the hole Russell's death created in the family. I ached for the loss. An otherwise happy moment with my children was a heart-wrenching, gut-stabbing experience for me.

I cried quietly so the children wouldn't hear. Tears spilled onto my cheeks; I couldn't stop the flow.

And then it hit me: *this* was my new normal.

The realization was so sudden, so brutal, I almost stepped on the brakes and crashed the car. This was not the happy, carefree life I'd envisioned for my new normal. It wasn't the life I desperately wanted.

"Normal" was living with the awful realization of what we'd lost. My family was getting on, moving forward. For me, the endless chasm left by Russell's passing would never go away, never be filled. Anytime I thought of his passing, I would be sad.

This new normal was awful! Anger rolled through me. I didn't want *this*. I wanted life to be *better*. I couldn't carry this pain for the rest of my life. The truth was bitter fruit. I wanted to spit it out to make it go away. But I couldn't. I had to carry this load for the rest of mortality.

Over time, I've slowly found ways to lighten the load by serving others and by trying to lift those who are suffering like I am. Just as others predicted, my mourning now, years after, isn't as sharp as it used to be. It isn't raw and all-encompassing anymore. Slowly, the load is getting lighter and the fruit less bitter. Maybe that just means my back is getting stronger and my mouth more accustomed to the taste.

For the first few years my grief surrounded me, penetrating everything like a fog. It obscured my view and impaired my ability to concentrate and think straight. As the fog cleared, my grief turned to a rage inside me. It screamed inside my brain and throughout my body. It replayed the gory details of Russell's death again and again so often I couldn't focus on anything else. It rubbed my emotions raw and would not let them rest. The grief was inexhaustible and never ending. The relentless torment felt so fierce I wanted to die.

Slowly, mercifully, that grief subsided. After the first few years, it slowly backed off. But the pain still visits from time to time with a force so shocking it instantly takes my breath away. I'm still aghast that those same emotions can be brought to the surface so quickly and completely, that I can relive the traumatic feelings from the day Russell died with such clarity, almost like the first time. Thankfully, this demon grief monster is no longer a resident here. It just visits now, never stays.

A new grief has come to take its place. This grief is my friend. She sits next to me when I'm alone. She puts her arms around me when I'm sad. She's quiet but she's always there. I have a feeling that this grief will never leave. She may step back when the demons come roaring into my brain, but she always reclaims her place when they go. This grief is gentle. Kind. Comforting.

I'm grateful she is here, although I'm not glad for the reason she is here. She stands by me, and together we peer into the dark, deep hole left in my life. She reminds me that it will not be filled in this life. That it *cannot* be filled. That a new baby wouldn't fill it. Work or service will not fill it. Spending money will not fill it. Not even God will fill it.

That the hole needs to be left empty so that one day Russell will be able to fill it again.

So I have stopped trying to fill the hole. I have stopped trying to make it better. Nothing can make this better, and that's okay. This experience has changed me; it has emptied me into nothingness and then filled me with something so much more meaningful. It has stretched and expanded me. Each step has hurt and will continue to hurt as I grow faster than I ever thought possible. But with that hurt comes a love and a gratitude so much deeper and far-reaching than I could ever have imagined.

No, my life will never be the same. Some days I look back at my old life with fondness—and a bit of jealousy. My new life, although different than expected, will lead to an amazing future that will last forever. And in that life, I will be together with my family. And then my holes will all be filled.

After Russell died, I reflected again on the changes I had seen in President Hinckley, thankful for the example he gave me and the rest of the Church in mourning the loss of a loved one. President Hinckley knew he was a well-beloved and much-watched man. He could have hidden his grief and acted like it didn't hurt as deeply as it did. He could have pretended and "moved on" much faster than he did. But he was honest. He could not lie and say this grief did not hurt.

President Hinckley took time to grieve. We saw his hurt because he was willing to share the depth of his pain with us. He was unpretentious. He was candid and sincere. He put himself in a vulnerable position that left him open to criticism. As a Church, we were generous in allowing him to grieve, although surely there were others as bewildered about it as I was.

I'm grateful to President Hinckley for being courageous enough to mourn freely over his wife. I'm grateful to see that even the man who was the mouthpiece for Jesus Christ struggled with his mortality and hurt terribly at the loss of his wife. If he could suffer that much, then I can too. President Hinckley showed me that it is okay to mourn, to slow down and be sad. To let some things go.

But he also showed me that life can continue, that it's okay to go on living, that the spark can come back. The spark hasn't quite come back for me yet, but I will patiently wait as I slowly return to life.

On January 27, 2008, President Hinckley quietly passed on through the veil. I'm sure all the past prophets were there to welcome him home and wish him a hearty congratulations on a life well lived. I bet they all got hugs and handshakes. But I wonder if he looked past them to find the one person he missed the most. In my mind, I see President Hinckley sweeping Sister Hinckley off her feet in the tightest embrace. It makes me smile to think about it, even if it also makes me a little jealous. I am happy that their short separation has ended.

I'm sure Russell saw their reunion. I'll have to ask him for all the details when it's my turn to join them on the other side.

# Chapter Nine
## MOTHER'S DAY

MY FIRST MOTHER'S DAY WAS fantastic. I couldn't wait to celebrate with my new baby girl! Karissa had just turned six months old. I can't remember what special things I planned for myself, but I remember the excitement of finally belonging to this day. I was a mom!

Juxtaposed against the experience I'd had just previous to becoming pregnant with Karissa, this was truly one of the happiest days of my life. This first Mother's Day was made all the more sweet because I had tasted the bitter not long before—when my dreams of becoming a mother became a nightmare of uncertainty and doubt.

Kirk and I had been married about a year and a half. We didn't really have the money to start a family, but we felt it was the right time, and I got pregnant right away. We were *so* excited! We planned and schemed about how we would tell the family. We dreamed about our new child and imagined the fun camping trips we would take together. We wondered whether we were having a boy or girl and thought about all of the new exciting and scary experiences we would have as parents. I was so happy to become a mom. I had many ideas about what I wanted to be when I grew up, but the one thing I knew for sure was that I would be a mom.

We made a funny video that announced the pregnancy, and we showed it to our extended family. We told them almost as soon as we found out ourselves. Soon all of our friends knew too.

Then I began to miscarry. I began bleeding, and the doctor put me on bed rest. Suddenly we had different news to share. We wished we hadn't been so exuberant, so excited, so loud so soon. I was scared. I was sad. I was bored. I was lonely. Most of all, I was unsure of the future. What if I did miscarry? Would I ever have kids? Would my body reject motherhood—the one thing I had looked forward to my whole life? For weeks these thoughts and concerns swirled around in my head. Was my worrying and stress negatively affecting the baby? Suddenly I was fearful of everything. Was it my fault I was losing this child?

It was maddening to be alone most of the day with my destructive thoughts, confined to my bed or the couch, unable to get up for anything more than to go to the bathroom. I became stir-crazy, but I was afraid to move.

Alone in our little one-bedroom duplex, I pled and cried. I tried to understand. I tried to hope and to have faith, but it was hard not knowing what to have faith in. Should I have faith in the pregnancy going full-term? If I had faith instead that I would get pregnant again later, would that show a lack of faith in this pregnancy? I read the scriptures. Unfortunately, too many of the stories dealing with pregnancy talked about years of infertility. I didn't want to read that.

Soon it was obvious we wouldn't be welcoming this child into our home. After I miscarried, I was destitute. I was drained. I was depressed. Knowing it was God's will did not help. Had I known then that we would have our five children relatively easily and relatively quickly from that point on, maybe I wouldn't have been so sad. The not knowing was the worst part.

Would we repeat this experience? Would we ever have children? Would I have to go through this nightmare every time we wanted to add a child to our family?

A few months later I did become pregnant. I walked on pins and needles, nervous for the first few months, afraid this pregnancy would end the same as the last. But this pregnancy was different. On November 11, 1996, our first child, Karissa Hess, was born, and six months later I had joined the ranks of those celebrating Mother's Day. My other Mother's Days were nice too, but none has been as memorable as my first.

* * *

The year Kirk was called as bishop, I was asked to speak on Mother's Day in sacrament meeting. I have two strong opinions about this. First, I have an extreme pet peeve about women speaking on Mother's Day. It's *our* day—the one time a year we get kudos for the hard work we do the other 364. Do we really have to anticipate it by writing and delivering a talk in front of hundreds? On Mother's Day, women should be able to sit in the front on the soft seats—all alone—so they can actually hear the talks while the husbands sit in the back with the kids, the chaos, and the Cheerios.

But to add insult to injury, I was the bishop's wife. I thought that when Kirk got the call, I'd be excused from giving talks for the next five years. We had five young children ranging from age ten to just over a year. Who in their right mind would think I'd be able to prepare a talk with all that craziness going on, let alone find someone to sit with my children while I sat on the stand?

I was not happy with this assignment. By now I knew that Mother's Day wasn't pleasant for every woman. Some women wanted to be moms but for different reasons hadn't been able to realize that dream. Some had lost children, and Mother's Day was a stark reminder that someone was missing. Other women had been estranged from their children, or their children were making bad choices. Many women felt guilty when they heard flowery remarks about how great mothers were supposed to be. I was somehow supposed to give a talk that would uplift and edify all of these women. And I was supposed to ponder and prepare for that talk in the middle of life's everyday pandemonium.

Not only did the assignment not sound easy or enjoyable, as Mother's Day loomed ahead, it didn't even look feasible.

I found I could not get a handle on where I wanted to go with my talk. I explored several different avenues, but nothing felt right. I thought about every aspect of motherhood I'd experienced, including the sadness and despair of my miscarriage. I finally decided to begin there, describing why the thought of Mother's Day had at one time been sad for me. Then I'd talk about the moms who felt inadequate, who felt like they were failing because they didn't fit the typical mold.

Most Mother's Day talks quote Alma 56:47–48, where Helaman recounts the bravery of the Anti-Nephi-Lehi youth. Helaman tells how these young men did not fear death—that the liberty of their fathers was more important than their own lives—and that "they [were] taught by their mothers, that if they did not doubt, God would deliver them."

We praise these stalwart mothers, who obviously did everything right to have raised such strong, committed boys. We assume these women were confident in their mothering skills—the June Cleavers of the Book of Mormon. We assume they knew how strong and brave their sons were. But this verse was written as a letter not from Helaman to the mothers but to Captain Moroni.

It's a fair assumption that these moms never heard the accolades written about them. They probably never knew what great moms they were.

In my preparation, I read a lesser-known verse about these moms written many chapters before—Alma 17:14. This verse described the type of people the sons of Mosiah went to convert. It was from these people that Helaman's stripling warriors eventually sprang: "They [the sons of Mosiah] had undertaken to preach the word of God to a wild and a hardened and a ferocious people; a people who delighted in murdering . . . and robbing and plundering."

The mothers of the stripling warriors came from this group. They had humbler and darker beginnings than we often give them credit for. Yet they turned their lives around and turned their hearts to God. They gave up the bad and embraced the good. I wonder if they still felt guilty for past sins. I wonder if they felt inadequate as they looked to their Nephite sisters who had grown up in the Church. I wonder if they would have ever believed that they'd be honored millennia later. I wonder if they would ever have imagined that *they* would become the goal, the unattainable bar of motherhood.

As I planned, prepared, and pondered, I felt rejuvenated in my love of being a mom. I realized that I'd taken much for granted. Preparing my talk refreshed my spirit. It enriched my soul. It helped me to see how fleeting this loud, noisy madness was and caused me to enjoy it more. The little things became fun again. I was able to laugh at the spills and take pleasure in the snuggles.

I didn't know it at the time, but it was my last Mother's Day with all of my children on earth. I had seven and a half months left to delight in a complete family. I could have spent those next seven and a half months very differently, being aggravated at the little things, being dissatisfied in the commotion and the mess, being stressed out by the noise and the bedlam.

But I didn't feel that way. Because I gave a talk that caused me to reevaluate the source of my happiness, I was able to revel in my family. I savored the moments more. I relished our time together and found satisfaction in our relationships.

I had no idea how important that experience would later be, of the impact it would have on my life—before and after Russell died. I didn't know how much I needed that talk and the preparation that went into it, but my Heavenly Father did. He gave me the assignment and then filled me with inspiration. I will forever be grateful for that last Mother's Day and for the talk that changed the course of my mothering at such a crucial point in my life.

\* \* \*

My heart hurts
I can't breathe
My body's full of dread
I try to breathe
I swallow hard
To clear my aching head
I blink back tears
And memories
That just won't go away
I miss my son
My little child
Who's not with me on this day
I start to cry
I want to die
My heart is ripping out
He's close at hand
Though I can't see
In this I have no doubt
I gasp for air
And close my eyes
There's lots I cannot say
I try to smile
And try not to cry
Happy Mother's Day.

The Mother's Day after Russell died, I didn't know what to do. I didn't feel like celebrating. The holiday came four and a half months after his death—far enough away that I felt like I had some small measure of control over my emotions but soon enough that the thought still stung. How did you celebrate being a mom when one of your children was missing?

As Mother's Day approached, I felt like I needed to prepare. I'd been dreading the day since sometime in February, when I first realized it was coming. I had no concrete plan, just a vague idea about how we should spend the day.

The children brought me the obligatory breakfast in bed. I opened all the handmade presents. I couldn't help but imagine that Russell was there too, watching with excitement, asking if he too could have some of my juice.

We went to church and listened to the flowery talks about mothers. I remember feeling numb—I didn't feel anything at all at first—and then a flood of emotion overpowered me and wrenched my soul. That day, two-year-old Joey didn't sit on my lap the entire meeting as he usually did. Now that he didn't have to fight with Russell for my lap, it was always where he seemed to be on Sundays. In fact, Joey would often get a book and back up to me, saying, "Lap, lap." I marveled at Joey's apparent disinterest in my lap as we sat there.

And I wondered if, instead, Russell was already sitting there and Joey was letting him stay without a fight.

\* \* \*

Mother's Day has changed for me over the years. The first year after Russell's death, it was a sad day—a painful reminder of what I had lost. The second year, I chose to ignore it and pretend it held no special significance to me. My refusal to acknowledge this holiday made it much worse for me and my children. Instead of being a happy celebration of motherhood, I was grumpy, and I think my kids were confused. The third year, I decided to face it head-on. I accepted that it was coming, and I decided to enjoy the day. Instead of letting my memories bring me down, I remembered them with a smile, grateful that I had them.

Now Mother's Day is not a reminder of what I lost, but it's a day to bask in the blessings of what I have now and what I had then.

# Chapter Ten
## A Song of the Heart

I AM AN ADEQUATE PIANO player. It has taken me years to reach that level, and I'm proud of it. But I have to work really hard at every song I play. The piano doesn't come naturally to me and never has. My earliest memories of piano lessons—or, I should say, my *only* memories of them—include the teacher berating me for not practicing. Of course, instead of inspiring me to practice more, I practiced even less—if that was possible—in retaliation.

Years later when I received my patriarchal blessing, it talked a little of my need to get back into music. It encouraged me to "learn again to love music."

*Great*, I thought. By then I couldn't even remember the right-hand notes.

On my mission I found a renewed interest in the piano. I realized how the power of music invited the Spirit and helped set the mood at meetings. Unfortunately, I attended many meetings without music because there was no one who could play. For the first time, I found myself wishing I had practiced and paid attention during my lessons.

After my mission, I dabbled as often as I could at the piano. I assumed I was too busy and too old to take lessons, so I tried to teach myself. Not being able to sight-read the notes, I worked for weeks trying to master a single hymn or Primary song. I wasn't *that* diligent, but after a long while, I had a handful of hymns and a few Primary songs under my belt. I still wouldn't play in front of people or—heaven forbid—when anyone was singing, but I was becoming more comfortable with playing.

I then married a piano teacher's son! We were at a baptism for a new member in our ward, and there was no one to play the piano. One of the members turned to me and said, "Well, you can play, can't you?" I mumbled about my lack of experience and ability. He turned to Kirk and said, "You mean you married someone who can't play the piano?"

That got me riled up enough to march to the front of the room and clumsily play the few hymns I could stumble through. It was painful—for me and for the ward members who had to sing so slowly, but playing that day broke down some barriers and fears, and I began practicing with a vengeance.

A few years later, I was asked to play a piece for the Primary choir in the stake Sing Noel program, a big deal in our city. Hundreds and hundreds of people come for two nights in December to listen to Christmas music and a message. The songs for Sing Noel were usually intricate and busy—meaning a fast tempo and lots of notes. I mumbled again about my lack of experience and ability, but the person on the other end would have none of it.

I worked on that song like I had never worked on a song before. It was tricky, and I had my doubts, but it was coming along. My biggest concern was playing in front of so many people.

I heard that our Primary was struggling to find a piano player, so I offered to play until they found one. That would give me practice in front of a forgiving group of people who probably wouldn't even notice that I was playing so many wrong notes. I wasn't even worried that I'd end up being called as the Primary pianist, because as a ward missionary I still had about six months left on my "mission." Boy, was I surprised when I was released early!

The Primary program was coming up, and the leaders expected me to play for it. I didn't know if I could, but as I got the list of songs, a miracle seemed to happen: I knew all of the songs except one—they were the songs I'd been dabbling with all the previous years. I shouldn't have been amazed, but I was. I had been inspired to learn them, on my own, just for fun, for the past six or seven years.

Even so, I was nervous about the program. I wasn't afraid of making a lot of mistakes—I expected that to happen. I was afraid of getting so freaked out, of messing up so much that I would run out of the chapel in tears. That became my goal: to *not* run out of the chapel.

During the program, my hands shook so bad it was hard to keep them over the keys. I played so many wrong notes that it was probably hard to tell what song I was playing. But I didn't run out. I met my goal and felt proud of myself.

The ironic thing about my piano career? The Sing Noel program decided the young women should sing the song I had been practicing for the Primary choir. They already had a pianist, so they didn't need me after all. I suddenly realized that Heavenly Father had really wanted me as Primary pianist, and though I felt that it was kind of a sneaky way to get me into it, it was probably the only way I would have let anyone in the Primary presidency know that I played. I only felt like I'd needed to play in the Primary program as practice to play in Sing Noel. Had I not received that phone call, I would not have gone looking to play the piano.

I enjoyed learning all of the Primary songs. I didn't get much better as a player, but I felt more confident, and my hands eventually stopped shaking. The other blessing was that I got to see all of my children each Sunday. I enjoyed watching my children in Primary as they grew.

I was able to see how Karissa and Kyle interacted with each other in senior Primary. They didn't sit next to each other but often waved to each other. I watched Jake interacting with his friends in junior Primary. Once, Russell ditched Nursery and sat in Primary with me. He spent most of the time waving and saying hi to Jake. While the junior Primary went to class and the senior Primary came in, I played prelude music to try to keep the peace. The big children came in laughing boisterously and saying things like, "Oh man, do you see *that*?" One of the counselors, who was pregnant to the point where she couldn't see her feet anymore, was standing at the front with her arms folded. We both looked at each other, surprised at the noise level.

Finally, I stood up to see what was causing the commotion. Russell, who had been sitting on the front row, was standing under the chorister's pregnant belly, out of her field of vision. He had pulled down his pants to his ankles and was mooning the entire senior Primary! I stopped playing, ran over to Russell, scooped up his naked body, pulled up his pants, and ran to the bathroom.

Russell became famous for this incident. He was proud of it, and his brothers were proud of him.

It may not rank high on my most proud moments in motherhood, but it does rank high as one of my funniest. I felt like I had this calling of Primary pianist so I could enjoy more of Russell before he was needed in heaven.

I was still the Primary pianist when he died. I hid behind the piano crying while I played the simple songs of heaven. The song leader couldn't look at me or she'd start crying too. One of the hardest days was just after we had celebrated what would have been Russell's fifth birthday, sixteen days after he died. That Sunday the song leader announced that we would be singing happy birthday to one of our special friends.

*Surely they wouldn't be singing to Russell*, I thought. But then Russell's best friend, Adam, stood up all proud and tall. In all my grief, I had forgotten it had been his birthday too. I could barely get through the song; I couldn't see the notes for the tears.

We had stake conference that next week. One of the congregational songs was "Now Let Us Rejoice."[10] I could barely squeak out the words, but I was mesmerized by that song. It was written by William W. Phelps and included in the Church's first hymnal in 1835. What hit me about this song was the thought of the people who originally sung it. They too had lost children. Life was hard and bleak at times. They were wading through the muck of despair and emptiness like I was. Maybe they also had a hard time being happy and were unable to feel the joy of the gospel. They were not rejoicing in their present experiences but in "the day of salvation."

I could do that. I knew that one day I would see and hug my Russell again. I could look forward to that day with joy even though the present offered me little. As I sang, I realized that these stalwart Saints and I had more in common than I'd ever thought. I found solace and comfort in the fact that we shared experiences and that they knew how hard this time was for me. They had been there, and worse. And still they could sing about rejoicing, for they had something marvelous to rejoice in. As I struggled to sing the last verse, I felt I needed to spend time playing the songs of the pioneers. I knew it would give me the added strength and feeling of joy that was absent in my life.

A few weeks after that, Kirk called me into the bishop's office and released me as Primary pianist. I figured it was purely out of necessity. I was obviously scaring the kids in Primary. The Relief Society didn't have a piano player, so I was put there. I was fine with that. There wasn't much I could do then anyway; I wasn't functioning well. I certainly couldn't teach; I couldn't even answer questions during Gospel Doctrine and Relief Society. I figured the change in calling solved two problems for the ward at once and kept me busy besides.

I had no idea how inspired and necessary this calling was for me.

I chose "Now Let Us Rejoice" as the opening song my first Sunday playing. I practiced it all week to be prepared, and the lyrics played all around in my head. During low times, I heard an angelic choir singing verse three:

> In faith we'll rely on the arm of Jehovah
> To guide thru these last days of trouble and gloom,
> And after the scourges and harvest are over,
> We'll rise with the just when the Savior doth come!
> Then all that was promised the Saints will be given
> And they will be crowned with the angels of heaven,
> And earth will appear as the Garden of Eden,
> And Christ and his people will ever be one!

The words lifted me in my time of need and brought me to higher ground. Having the song in my head helped me to rejoice in a future I knew I would someday experience. It kept me in a better emotional state for longer.

I hadn't been able to listen to the radio or watch television much since Russell died; both added too much confusion and noise. And since my brain was empty of current events or rock songs, the hymns I was practicing for Relief Society stayed in my head all day long. I often found myself humming them or thinking the words without even realizing it. When negative thoughts swirled around my brain, a phrase from a hymn would appear out of nowhere, reminding me of the purpose of life.

This isn't to say that I never felt sad. I felt sad all the time. At times I felt so depressed I couldn't think of the hymns. Sometimes I didn't *want* to think of the hymns. I didn't want their comfort or companionship, and many times I didn't allow them to break my reverie. But there were so many times I needed those hymns—just a line or two was enough—to motivate me to get up, get out of bed, and move forward.

One day, about seven months after Russell died, I was out running by myself. I didn't run alone often, but that day I felt like I could. I was running up a big hill when I was assaulted with the image of Russell dying in the emergency room. I felt as if I had been physically hit in the stomach and chest. I couldn't breathe. I couldn't think straight. The pain was so intense I thought I was having a heart attack. I'd already had quite a few panic attacks, but this one was a doozy. I had to stop running and sit down. My throat constricted, and although I was breathing, I felt like no air was getting in. My lungs burned, and I was swooning. The images of the past became sharper, violently forcing themselves into my mind.

*You're breathing*, I told myself. *You're not choking. It's all in your head.* Finally the pictures faded. My breathing slowed from a frantic, frenzied pace to a controlled, natural one. My vision cleared, and I could see the present instead of the past. As I got up, I became aware of the lyrics of "How Firm a Foundation," which had been quietly playing in the recesses of my mind, specifically the fourth verse:

When through the deep waters I call thee to go,
The rivers of sorrow shall not thee o'erflow,
For I will be with thee, thy troubles to bless,
And sanctify to thee, And sanctify to thee,
And sanctify to thee thy deepest distress.[11]

I had been working on it for Relief Society. It had four flats and was tricky for a novice like me. I of course liked the song, but I didn't realize how I'd internalized it until it came to my rescue and pulled me out of one of my most severe panic attacks.

And I hadn't thought my calling as pianist was inspired.

I've come to realize that Heavenly Father was filling *me* by putting me in what I'd thought were seemingly insignificant positions. A God who could see the beginning and the end and *everything* in between, a God who knew my heart, was giving me, through music, the tools I needed to help myself in my time of trouble and deepest distress.

## Chapter Eleven
### RUSSELL ROCKS

IT WAS OUR FIRST ROAD trip without Russell, just a month and a half after his death. We started in Death Valley and ended up in the Calico ghost town with several stops in between. I felt it was too soon to travel without him, but Kirk and the children were excited for a new adventure.

I found I wasn't as sad on the road; there were new things to see—things that didn't remind me of Russell. New experiences kept my mind engaged and not focused on my old ones. I still missed Russell terribly, but the pain wasn't as excruciating. The fog lifted a little so I could see other things. It was a brief respite from the engulfing, suffocating grief. Kirk loves a new adventure and took us on many trips that first year. It's one of the things that really helped me make it through that first year full of those heart-wrenching *firsts*.

Coming home from each trip, though, was a different experience. Starting for home I felt light and well rested. The closer we got to home, however, as I started recognizing places, a sadness would descend upon me again, making me want to cry. Memories flooded my mind and ripped at my heart. Breathing became increasingly hard.

The first time this happened I wondered what was wrong with me; I'd been doing so well! But there I was in the car, reduced again to an emotional disaster, unable to function, unable to cope.

On succeeding trips, I recognized the gloom settling in on the return home and didn't feel quite as helpless as it surrounded me and tried to overcome my spirit. I could do nothing about the heaviness, but anticipating it and recognizing it as a normal part of my grief helped me prepare for it. When I was ready for it, the pain wasn't as crushing or smothering. At first the grief was hard and unyielding, like being rolled under the tire of a semitruck. Later it became more like a pile of heavy blankets being laid on me. But although it lessened in weight, it always came.

On later trips, I felt Russell's closeness and realized that he'd joined us, but on that first trip, I just felt empty. We stopped at our campsite in Death Valley, and I sat on the rocks, watching Joey while Kirk and the other children set up our camping trailer. I missed Russell so much; monstrous teardrops splashed down my cheeks and onto the rocks at my feet. I looked down, watching the trail of tears, when something miraculous caught my eye. There at my feet was a big heart-shaped rock. It was about the size of both of my fists put together. I'd never seen a heart-shaped rock, let alone one so large. I gazed at it, awestruck. Instinctively I looked up, searching for Russell. Surely he'd snuck past me and had put the rock there when I wasn't looking. The thought felt so plausible: he'd left me a token of his love. Russell loved rocks; I could see him carefully shaping this one for me.

That trip, we camped in several locations, giving me more chances to search for more heart-shaped rocks. I was amazed at how many I found. With each discovery, my heart did a little leap and then melted a little as I picked up another one. The rocks felt warm in my cool hand, and I liked to feel for the point or trace the groove of the heart's apex.

I started looking for heart rocks on all of our trips. Thinking that Death Valley was a special, singular gift, I didn't expect to find any more. But I found more and more. Soon I became obsessive, constantly looking down as we hiked, searching desperately for more signs of Russell's love.

After a while, I knew I had enough Russell rocks and shouldn't look anymore, but I couldn't stop myself. They were something tangible, something I could see and hold. My arms ached for Russell, the muscle memory in them missing his weight and form. The rocks were a poor substitute, but they were *something*.

I continued searching for "Russell rocks." I told myself that Russell was busy, that I couldn't expect him to take the time to leave more rocks for me, that it was time to move on, and that I didn't need a sign to know that Russell loved me and was still active in my life. Yet my eyes were drawn to the ground, always looking. If I didn't find a heart rock within the first half mile of a hike, panic seized me. I would frantically scan the ground, crying in my heart, *I'm not ready to let go.*

Mentally I pled with Russell, with Heavenly Father, to give me more rocks. I always found another. I was never let down.

I felt a bit silly and embarrassed at my insatiable need, at my inability to walk away without a token from Russell. I felt like an addict, unable to survive without my rocks. *I'll be okay without them*, I told myself—a hollow lie, and I knew it. I needed those rocks like I needed to breathe.

One time, more than a year after Russell died, we were hiking to the Bridge to Nowhere in the Angeles Mountains. At the trailhead I saw a *huge* heart-shaped rock the size of a watermelon. I pointed it out to Karissa, who was just as amazed as I was. I couldn't pick it up then and carry it the whole way because it was so heavy, but I could carry it out of the park after our hike—provided some other hiker didn't find it and take it first.

*It's okay if it's not there when we get back*, I thought. But the entire hike—even while I was putting other smaller heart-shaped rocks in my backpack—I thought of that rock.

When we finally returned, the big rock was still there. I hefted it, surprised at its weight. Arms aching but heart rejoicing, I hiked uphill with it for the last mile. What a find!

When we got home, I weighed the rock just for kicks. Twenty-three pounds!

*Okay, I have a problem*, I thought. But I didn't care—I had the coolest Russell rock ever!

The compulsion to find rocks had many parallels to my life. I was constantly looking down, looking for Russell. While looking down, I saw dirt, grass, rocks—the low things in my life. I was missing beautiful vistas—the trees and the mountains ahead. The problem of being stuck in the past or the dreary present is that it becomes almost impossible to look forward and see what the future holds.

But I couldn't look up. Trying to plan, to imagine, or to dream a future without Russell was too hard. I survived minute by minute, day to day. I couldn't even think about tomorrow, next week or—heaven forbid—next year.

On my worst days, not even Russell rocks offered me solace. I was mad at them.

*I've lost my child*, my mind roared, *and all I've got to show for it is a handful of rocks*? I wanted to rage. To throw those rocks and break something. To throw them far, far away in anger and disgust. But I never did. I was too afraid. I couldn't sever that last physical tie I had with my son. I knew it wasn't a real tie, but it was all I had.

On my good days, I was grateful for my cowardice. That's when the rocks made me smile. I have them stashed all over my house and hiding in pockets. On good days, they're like special surprises that keep me going. On bad days, I try to ignore the rocks and wait for my mood to improve.

Over time, I found I wasn't as tied to the rocks as I used to be. Sometimes I'd forget to look for rocks at the beginning of a hike. Then I'd remember—and feel the old frenzied desire to find one.

*I'll stop looking after the first anniversary*, I promised myself. But when the one-year mark came, I still had the voracious need to find my special Russell rocks.

Then, one day, just Kirk and I went hiking, about a year and a half after Russell's angel day—the day Russell became an angel. I already had a few heart rocks tucked away in my pocket. Kirk had gone ahead, and I was alone on the trail. I wasn't thinking of Russell. I was thinking of a Mother's Day talk a friend had given a few weeks before. She had one school-age child and had suffered many miscarriages. She openly and poignantly shared her struggles with being the mother of one when she had planned to be the mother of many. It was an honest and heartfelt talk, one that touched me deeply.

I thought about her pain and her courage to share such a sensitive part of her life with the congregation. I was reflecting on her emotional distress instead of mine when I saw it: a beautiful, white, perfectly formed, heart-shaped rock. It looked almost like a crystal, thin and striking—perfect for my collection.

But I knew immediately that this rock was meant for another grieving mother, not me.

Giving it up was hard, but it was a step toward letting go and healing. Once I decided to give that rock to my friend, I thought of another friend who was going through chemo for breast cancer. Maybe I could find a heart rock for her too. After walking for a few more minutes, I found it.

Giving away heart rocks lessened my attachment and need for them. I admit I still look for Russell rocks, and I still find them. They hold a special place in my heart. But I'm calmer now, and my compulsion has gone away. The frantic feeling has been replaced with a special kind of strength, the strength to say good-bye to Russell, the strength to move forward.

And the strength to look up.

## Chapter Twelve
### JOSEPH SMITH

I HAD ALWAYS FELT A closeness to Joseph Smith. I admired his diligence, his strength, and his ability to stay true to the things he believed despite heart-wrenching trials and heavy burdens. I loved hearing the story of how he went off in the woods to pray to find out directly from God which church he should join. But when I went on my mission, I started seeing how far-fetched that story might sound. I wasn't sure I would be able to share it with others.

Secretly, I decided I wouldn't teach Joseph's First Vision because it sounded too unreal and could lead to too many questions—and doubts. But I didn't feel comfortable with my decision, so I began searching out scriptures I could use that would "prove" why I believed my church to be led by God. I found some scriptures, but there wasn't enough evidence to sway a doubter.

In desperation, I followed the example of Joseph Smith and took my dilemma to the Lord. I told Him of my fears, my inadequacies, my lack of knowledge. The answer I got wasn't what I expected. I wanted proof, concrete evidence that would stop someone cold. Something that could not be refuted. Something that sounded normal—not like fantasy.

The Lord quietly told me that He'd called Joseph Smith in this special way to lead this last dispensation. If I truly believed and shared that belief with someone who truly was searching for the truth, the Holy Ghost would touch that person's heart in a way that would help them know it was true. No matter how strange it might sound to our ears, the story of a fourteen-year-old boy who knelt down in a grove of trees to pray to his Father in Heaven and who saw God the Father and Jesus Christ as a result was true. I knew it. I could feel it deep within my heart and throughout my entire being.

I felt, as a result of *my* prayer, that if I refused to share this tender story because of my fear of man, I would not only offend God, but I would also miss the opportunity to help lead someone to the truth.

So I talked about the First Vision at every opportunity. Whenever I quoted Joseph's words from his testimony, the reaffirming power of the Holy Ghost touched me and filled me with love. I realized that I loved Joseph Smith. I was proud of him for sharing this story no matter how unreal it might sound. We have so much more knowledge about life, about death, about the plan of our Heavenly Father because Joseph Smith was brave enough to talk about an experience he'd had and then live true to it.

Sure, I was mocked at times for telling people about the First Vision, but a bond had formed between me and Joseph Smith. I trusted him and the scriptures that came through him. I believed his words and was curious about his life. I read books and tried to learn more about this amazing man.

Though he had little to work with, Joseph tried to live the best he could. He suffered much distress and pain in his short life, and yet he persevered. He performed the labor his Heavenly Father had called him to do. Joseph faced the challenges of the prophets of old. Like Moses and Abraham, he had to contend not only with unbelievers who were offended at his teachings but also with the disenchanted who lost their testimonies and chose to fight the Church.

I could see why Joseph had to seal his testimony with his blood—to die a martyr's death—to prove how deeply he believed. That I could understand.

But one trial in Joseph's life I could *not* understand.

From the day I first began my kinship with Joseph, I was troubled with the fact that he and his wife, Emma, had lost six of their eleven children. It seemed unfair and disproportionate for the Smith family to have so great a number of losses when compared to the amount of service they gave to the kingdom. I could not understand why a loving Heavenly Father allowed Joseph and Emma to lose so many children. It was a part of Joseph's history that caused me sadness and serious reflection. Wasn't it enough that he was giving his entire life, his entire being to his beliefs? Wasn't it enough that he was harassed and jailed unjustly? That he was hunted and maltreated? That he worked tirelessly with the time that he had to build the kingdom of God? Why was it necessary that he should suffer *this* way? Why couldn't he have his children at his side in this life?

It seemed to me unjust. Almost heartless. But unjust and heartless were not traits of the Heavenly Father I knew. Which was why I could never comprehend that after the countless trials Joseph Smith and his family endured, they had to suffer the loss of so many children.

I don't think it was by chance that our Relief Society and priesthood curriculum the year Russell died came from *Teachings of the Presidents of the Church: Joseph Smith*. As I thumbed through the new manual the first Sunday after Russell's angel day, I was filled again with awe, admiration, and love for the man who had given much so that we could have much. I skimmed the chapter headings and knew it would be good for me to learn more about his life.

At chapter fourteen, I stopped cold. The title was "Words of Hope and Consolation at the Time of Death." It was the first chapter I read, and as I read it, understanding replaced the confusion that had plagued me regarding the untimely deaths of so many of the Smith children.

Prophets receive revelation from God for the Church and the world. They know what we need to hear. They know what we need to do to be prepared for the calamities that come to us. If we heed the prophets' direction, we will be ready for what is ahead. I have noticed, however, that along with this inspiration, prophets also get revelation specific to *their* hardships, questions, and ponderings.

Joseph Smith was no exception. It must have been heartrending for him and his family to lose child after child, most succumbing to death shortly after birth. Emma and Joseph laid to rest six of their eleven children.

I imagine that Joseph spent many hours on his knees, pleading with the Lord for answers. I know how hard it has been for me to lose *one* of my five children. I can't even begin to imagine the pain and torture he and Emma experienced. And yet they were able to move forward and stay strong in their fledgling religion. They were both able to do so much good, even with so much loss.

Not only were they able to give much-needed consolation to the mourning Saints of their day, but the words of Joseph Smith regarding death and the life hereafter also give great comfort and solace to those of us who live so many years later.

Said he, "What have we to console us in relation to the dead? We have reason to have the greatest hope and consolation for our dead of any people on the earth."[12]

Of greatest consolation to me are the words of Joseph regarding the death of children. At the funeral of a two-year-old child, Joseph said:

We have again the warning voice sounded in our midst, which shows the uncertainty of human life; and in my leisure moments I have meditated upon the subject and asked the question, why it is that infants, innocent children, are taken away from us, especially those that seem to be the most intelligent and interesting. . . . The Lord takes many away, even in infancy, that they may escape the envy of man, and the sorrows and evils of this present world; they were too pure, too lovely, to live on earth; therefore, if rightly considered, instead of mourning we have reason to rejoice as they are delivered from evil, and we shall soon have them again. . . . Notwithstanding all this glory, we for a moment lose sight of it and mourn the loss, but we do not mourn as those without hope.[13]

He also said, "A question may be asked—'Will mothers have their children in eternity?' Yes! Yes! Mothers, you shall have your children; for they shall have eternal life, for their debt is paid."[14]

Joseph Smith also taught that parents who lose young children will have the joy, the pleasure, and the satisfaction of rearing those children after the resurrection until they have reached the full stature of their spirits. And he said it would be much more joyous than raising those children in life because we will be free from the sorrow and fear and disabilities of mortal life.

Joseph Smith was not immune to loss. He suffered at least as much, if not more, than many of his contemporaries. And so he could grieve with them. He knew their suffering because he too was suffering. He could console because, although he was sitting in the mire with them, he could see what was to come. He could lift and enlighten, and that power has reached across time to touch all of us who have come after.

At times, Joseph Smith wept. His heart was torn. I'm sure his spirit was depressed. I have grieved for him as I've read of his many losses. With Joseph, I find I grieve with a kindred spirit. Through him, I have learned much about perseverance and moving forward through agony and pain.

In reading Joseph Smith's "Words of Hope and Consolation at the Time of Death," I realized one reason why God allowed Joseph Smith to lose so many children. For me. As arrogant and self-adulating as this may sound, what I mean is this: because Joseph Smith lost so many children, he pled. He reflected. He pondered. He prayed. I am the recipient of the wealth of knowledge he received as he waded through the anguish of loss. I am not grateful that the Smith family lost so many children, but I *am* grateful that he gained so much inspiration and insight and was able to share it with me and others like me. His loss has made my loss easier to bear.

It's been a comfort to see how Joseph Smith could get through the oppressive bog of grief and still continue on. It is an example that gives me strength and the courage to get out of bed each morning and to keep moving. The solace I receive from reading Joseph's writings about loss, death, and the eternities beyond brings joy and hope to my heart. It makes me smile and love this great man even more.

With the knowledge I've gained from Joseph Smith also comes the responsibility to do as he did: to mourn with those who also have lost and to share with them the same words of hope and consolation. Through Joseph Smith, I've learned of the beauty that is promised me if I live right. Through me and those who have been touched by the prophetic words of Joseph Smith, others may also behold and experience the beauty of eternal life.

# Chapter Thirteen
## CHOICES

ABOUT A YEAR AFTER RUSSELL'S death, my brother-in-law showed me a cool new application on his cell phone. After inputting my present health history—height, weight, how often I exercised—he started asking me a few obscure health questions. How many living grandparents did I have? How old were they? What major diseases ran in my family? How often did I floss?

He recorded every answer, pushed enter, then turned to me with a grin. "You have forty-seven more years left to live!" he said triumphantly. Taken aback, I smiled politely and turned away.

*Forty-seven more years?* I wanted to cry. I'd already lived a year more than I'd wanted to. But forty-seven more? That meant I wasn't even halfway done with my life! I could barely look into next week, let alone next year. But *forty-seven more* years? It was too much to bear. And yet there was nothing I could do about it. I couldn't stop exercising—when I wasn't consistently exercising, my lows became lower, my depression more severe. I had no control over how long my grandparents lived or over the major diseases in my family's history. Apparently, flossing was the only thing I could control.

Maybe when I get closer to the other end of that dreaded forty-seven years I'll be glad I was given so many extra after Russell died. But even now it seems overwhelming and too much for me to handle.

Oh, and by the way, I have stopped flossing.

\* \* \*

I'm not really sure who I am anymore. Before Russell died, I knew myself pretty well. I had a lot of energy back then. At least, I think I did. I was much more spontaneous. I was genuinely happy. Happy with who I was and where I was in life. Even though things didn't always go my way, even when the children were fighting or crying, even when dinner was burning on the stove and the house was a disaster. I was a happy person even through those frustrating times. I enjoyed my life. I enjoyed my family. We played together and laughed together. That last fact gives me great solace now that one of my children is missing.

Not that my life was always rosy. I was an incredibly ornery teenager who liked to argue and prove how right I was in any situation. My parents were convinced I'd be a lawyer—and a successful one at that. I got mad and held grudges. I was confrontational and never backed down.

It took me years of growing up to realize that I didn't like that part of myself. I might have been victorious after a squabble, but I felt empty and deflated. The spoils became meaningless and gave little satisfaction. Unfortunately, it took too much time after that realization to claim ownership of the bad feelings. I argued with myself—successfully, for a while—that it wasn't *my* fault I felt bad. If the other person had acted differently, we wouldn't have fought in the first place.

Slowly I began to realize that if I wanted to feel better about myself, I'd have to change *me*.

But it was a challenge. It was a struggle not to say things I wanted to say. When biting my tongue didn't seem to be enough, I forced myself to think one positive thing about the person or situation. I made myself review the other person's point of view before responding. I had to reprogram the automatic thoughts and responses that had developed over the years. But I was able to do it. Slowly—ever so slowly—and with much backsliding, my automatic thoughts and responses changed. They became more positive. I became understanding.

Later I realized that my reactions had become more Christlike and that I was becoming more Christlike.

This generosity toward others made me more generous with myself. I began to genuinely like who I was—warts and all. I could relax and laugh at myself and not worry if others were laughing at me too. When I saw faults in others, instead of criticizing their weaknesses, I would often think, "Huh, I do that too. Maybe I should work on that." While little annoyances (and big annoyances) still had the potential to get my hackles up, my newly programmed thoughts usually calmed me down.

I wasn't perfect by any means, but I'd come a long way. Maybe an outsider wouldn't feel that I was as nice and generous as I am making myself out to be, but I felt like I'd changed. I was working on it, and I saw the change working within me.

When the children first came along I sometimes found myself getting uptight when they were always crying, hanging on me, and making huge messes. Again, I had to take a deep breath and remind myself of the big picture. It took some retraining, but, again, it worked. By the time Russell came around, I felt like I'd made it. Sure, I lost my temper from time to time, but most days we enjoyed ourselves. Because I worked so hard to make our home life more enjoyable, I thankfully have no regrets about the time I spent with Russell when he was alive. I can look back without apology or remorse. I still have acute sorrow stirred up by the loss and loneliness I feel without him, but I also feel a sense of satisfaction that I did my best for him while he was here.

After Russell died, the old me started sneaking back in. Small irritations seemed overwhelming, and I would lose my temper. The house felt too loud and too messy to handle, yet I didn't have the strength or energy to fix it. I found I didn't like the type of person I was becoming.

While I realized that I owned my feelings and was the only one who could change them, I also realized I was tired, and it just seemed like changing would take so much effort. I was grumpy that along with all of the other things I had to deal with, I also had to deal with character flaws I'd already fixed and tweaked years before. It was as though this harrowing experience really had *harrowed* me—it had ripped me apart and stripped me to the bone until I was nothing. As I tried to make sense of my new self, I found it nearly impossible. I was constantly changing—a chameleon who could not control my emotions. With no other recourse, I made a concentrated effort to control my negative emotions from spilling into our family dynamic. I'd done it before and knew I could do it again. That was some consolation.

I knew I could control my thoughts for the most part, so that's where I started. I tried again to come up with at least one positive thought for each person or situation I encountered. I tried again to see things from other people's points of view. I became more generous to the thoughtless comments sent my way as I remembered the inadequacies and fears that had engulfed me when my neighbors' children died. I went out of my way to talk to people who were afraid to talk to me. It all required a conscious, vigorous effort, and it sometimes drained me.

But I was happy about who I was choosing to be.

And yet I still didn't know who I was. I was still changing so much, so often. I wasn't *me* yet, and I didn't want to get to know this pseudo-me who would just morph into someone else by next week. So I stayed a stranger to myself and, I'm sure, to everyone else. I talked to myself, contemplating how I was getting through the mire. I was introspective yet distanced from making any friendships with the stranger in the mirror. Sometimes I watched my reactions like an outsider. I wasn't critical, but I gave myself an informed opinion on my actions and thoughts.

The stranger was like a knot, and I was patiently untying it to see what I would be left with. Some loops surprised me, and some tangles made me pity this poor, messed-up creature. Sometimes I had to put the knot down because it seemed the jumbled mass was twisted and snarled beyond repair. I let myself grieve and weep. I didn't force myself up; I just waited until the time seemed right and I was ready to pick up that seemingly impossible intertwined piece of my psyche and slowly begin again to work it free.

Enough time has now passed that the real me is beginning to take shape. It's taken over two years to get here. I still have a lot of choices ahead about how I want to react to situations. I realized not long ago that I could become anybody or anything I chose. That thought invigorated and inspired me, but at the same time it filled me with an inexpressible horror of the responsibility of it all.

*I* decide. Who I become is up to *me*. I can't blame anyone or anything—not even the death of my child—on how I decide to respond. I'm not talking about depression. I'm not talking about the inability to function after a traumatic event. I'm talking about what I choose to do with it. Sometimes my depression takes hold of me, and I am not able to take action. I'm talking about when I feel strong enough to make a choice, or when I don't necessarily *feel* strong enough but I know it is time to act.

When about two years had passed since Russell's death, people stopped being as gentle with me. It wasn't that they'd forgotten my grief; it was just that they didn't think about it during conversations with me or during lessons in church like they had before. I noticed more than ever how the loss of a child had estranged me from "regular" people, and in many ways that bothered me.

I became impatient with speakers who talked about trials that seemed insignificant to me. I became angry when I heard someone else's trial being resolved happily. I felt bitter. I didn't like the way this soured my heart. I felt the need to stew about it and vent to others. I knew I shouldn't gossip, but the need to share my perceived injustices overwhelmed me at times.

After listening to a speaker at a women's conference explain the different stages of grief, I learned something about myself. During her presentation, she shared that she'd never experienced profound grief herself—and that enraged me. How could she teach about grief when she hadn't been through it? I tried to be nice, but my body language probably showed my irritation. Afterward, I fumed about her presentation and said some regrettable things.

At home, I reassessed my behavior—and was embarrassed. Why was I so angry with a person who knew the information by the book but not necessarily through experience? I was jealous of her. I had been her once upon a time—innocent and naive. But that me had died and was buried with Russell. I would never have that innocence back, and I now coveted it in others. My resentment of people who hadn't suffered loss or experienced great affliction masked my jealousy. I knew I was angry with people who had minimal problems. But I didn't realize until after the women's conference that it was jealousy that created the feelings of anger in me. I was envious of the simplicity of their lives, and that envy manifested itself in bitterness and a great need to tear down. When I recognized my tendency to anger for what it was, I knew I needed to stop it. I may not have been able to change the way I *felt* about a person's message, but I could change the way I *reacted* to it. For me, changing my reaction was easier when I understood *why* I felt the way I did.

I often assume I know what other people's lives are like. If they have a happy disposition, I automatically believe they have not experienced profound grief or loss, that I can't relate to them because I have lost my innocence. These incorrect judgments have altered the way I've perceived others, and I've missed out on valuable friendships and service opportunities simply because I've formed inaccurate opinions about these people.

I began to notice that everyone struggled through trials. Some trials might seem trivial to me, but they didn't seem trivial to the one trying to resolve them. Not everyone experienced loss in the same way I had, but as I looked around I saw that everyone experienced loss on varying levels. Everyone hurt and everyone grieved at different times in their lives. I may not have been privy to their personal struggles, but I did know they were also having a mortal experience, and this knowledge helped me to be less judgmental.

This brought me to a crossroads. It was up to me to decide which way to go, and I found it strange that I was finally strong enough to choose: I could be the mopey, bitter woman who refused to stop wallowing in her depression or the woman with the happy disposition, the one people assume has never suffered. I wanted to be genuinely happy again, and I knew it wouldn't be possible if I allowed jealousy and anger to rule my life. But I feared the higher road. I was afraid that when people looked at me they would never suspect the deep chunk that was missing from my life; I was afraid that when people looked at me, they wouldn't see *me*.

There seemed to be no middle ground. I couldn't have a happy disposition while wallowing in my pain. I knew which woman I *should* become, but I didn't know if I wanted to let go of my resentment and become her.

I'm still figuring out who I am. It's taking longer than I ever anticipated, and I am starting to see that I may never fully solve the puzzle. There are permanent aspects of me, though, that I am starting to accept and even appreciate.

*I am a bereaved mother*, and I hurt every day.

*I am a wife*, and I love my husband.

*I am a mom.* I can love my living children while missing my little missionary. I can enjoy seeing Karissa, Kyle, Jake, and Joey together without Russell. I can hold them without feeling bad that I will never again hold Russell in this life. I can even laugh at their silliness and jokes without comparing them to Russell's pranks.

*I am a daughter of God*, and I am thankful for the plan He prepared for me. I am amazed beyond measure, even astonished at the ornate planning this has taken since the beginning of time. *Grateful* doesn't even begin to describe what I feel for Him. In fact, there are no words that can ever describe the feelings of my heart for my Heavenly Father and my Savior, Jesus Christ, and for this plan They created so that I could be reunited with my family.

So right now, today, this is who I am. I'm still figuring out the details, but the important pieces of me are in place. If I remain true to these truths that I know, the rest of me will someday emerge. I'll continue to morph and to change—that's part of why I'm here. But I'm becoming comfortable again in my own skin. I'm getting to know myself again, and I'm choosing to make myself someone I can be proud of.

## Chapter Fourteen
### BEAUTY FOR ASHES

"To appoint unto them that mourn in Zion, to give unto them
beauty for ashes, the oil of joy for mourning, the garment of
praise for the spirit of heaviness; that they might be called trees
of righteousness, the planting of the Lord, that he might be
glorified."

—Isaiah 61:3

MY LIFE WAS FULL OF ashes after Russell died, but through the grieving
process, I was given a beauty that I had never before experienced. I was
anointed with an oil of joy from my family and friends, who desperately
wanted to take away my pain. I had a spirit of heaviness that lightened
when I turned away from my grief and tried to alleviate the pain of another.
Seeds of hope sprouted and began to grow inside my heart as I looked to
my Lord for help.

We buried Russell on January 7, 2008. Although it was a bleak day,
it was also a good day. Some of my neighbors wanted to come but were
worried about bringing their children who had been Russell's friends.
They anticipated a somber and depressing service. I tried to explain that
we would be celebrating Russell's short life, not bemoaning it. This was to
be a "graduation party," a day we could smile at the memories.

The tables in the foyer depicting Russell's life showed a happy boy, full of
personality and a zest for life. His drawings, costumes, and stuffed animals
were all on display, along with family pictures and special memories.

The funeral itself was beautiful. The talks, poems, and musical
numbers were just right. Kirk's magnificent talk amazed me. I felt blessed
to be married to such an inspired man and to have had Russell in my
family. I felt complete that day. My husband and *all* five children were
there. I hadn't felt Russell close until that day, but I knew he was there,

and I knew it would be the last time we would all be together for a while. I hadn't been able to say good-bye, really, at the hospital, and now I could. I reveled in the completeness of my family. As I tried to slowly let Russell go, I found I could smile through my tears. I felt a sense of closure.

The month of January was kind of a wash. We were all reeling from the shock of Russell's death and struggling with the finality of it all. One minute he was here with us—we could see him, smell him, hear him, hold him—the next minute he was just gone. Vanished. Like a ghost. He had no substance, no form. He was just a memory—or was it only a dream? It was so sudden, so unexpected, so final. We each had to come to terms with Russell's absence and try to figure out the new family dynamic.

Besides the regular day-to-day stuff, there were individual needs each of my children had. It was important to Jake that I continue to help in his class. It gave him comfort and a sense of normalcy to see me at school on my volunteer day.

Karissa wanted me to give her my whole attention when she told me about her day. It was exhausting at times to try to keep up with the fast-paced scenarios of sixth grade. I did my best to smile and to remember all of the information she was throwing at me.

Joey wanted to be outside. I took him to the park often, even though it exposed me to new people and other moms who wanted to chat about their children and ask questions about mine.

Kyle was chafing under my newfound anxieties and needed the space to try crazy things. He was also nine, and a boy. He wanted to see how high he could climb, how far he could jump, and what other feats his body would allow him to accomplish. Kyle wanted me to let him be daring, which was by far the hardest thing for me to do for any of my children. I wanted to rein him in, keep him safe. I saw the worst-case scenario every time he attempted something. For the most part, I kept my mouth shut. I kept my thoughts to myself. Sometimes I even had to walk away. I didn't want my irrational fears to squelch the independence I saw in Kyle.

It felt good to give my family what I could. I still cried every day, I still struggled to breathe, I was still consumed with grief, and I didn't seem to have strength for me, but I found I had the strength for them.

One night, we were sitting on the living room floor playing a board game. I don't remember the game or any of the conversation, but I remember all of us laughing and enjoying being together. As I looked at Kirk and each of my children, a thought floated softly into my mind.

We're going to make it.

\* \* \*

Five months after Russell's angel day, a girl in Karissa's class lost her father. He died suddenly, just weeks after being diagnosed with cancer. Kyle knew this girl's brother, and although neither he nor Karissa knew the children well, they wanted to do something for them.

Our family sat down together to brainstorm ideas. We had a special empathy for this family. We knew how hard it had been for us those first months, and we'd had a lot of support. We talked about all of the things people had done for us and tried to decide what we could do for them that would be helpful and meaningful.

One practical and thoughtful gift we'd received was a month's worth of lunch tickets for each of my kids. I never bought school lunch for my kids, so this was a special treat for them. It was also meaningful to me because making lunches every morning before school was one less thing I had to worry about. We gave the grieving family a month's worth of lunch tickets for each of the children, and later I made each of them a memory quilt to remember their dad by.

Helping another family who had also lost a loved one was healing for us. Serving someone else made our wound less painful, and it gave us a sense of purpose. It gave Russell's death a sense of purpose.

In the years following Russell's death, I have become acquainted with many others who have survived the death of a loved one. I know there is nothing I can say that will take the grief away or make it better, but I also know that just doing something can soften the sting. It takes away some of the sting in my life too.

I knew that the family would probably be inundated with food and invitations to call "if you need anything," so I brought what was most helpful to me those first numb-filled days: a basket for the cards, a notebook to write things down in, and a big hug with the promise that while it never goes away, it does get better.

\* \* \*

Holidays without Russell topped the list of days that were the worst, but I *expected* those days to be bad. Second on the list were the days I didn't see coming.

At the beginning of summer break, I took all of my children with me to the orthodontist for Karissa's and Kyle's appointments. The orthodontist seemed extra chatty that day and asked what felt like a strangely worded

question: "How many children will you have home with you this summer?"
She looked up from Karissa's braces, waiting for an answer.

I turned the question around in my head for a moment, fumbling for
an answer. I would only have four children home with me this summer.

*But I have five kids.*

But I would only have four of them home with me this summer.

*But I have five kids.*

She looked at me expectantly, and I meekly answered, "Four."

Satisfied, she began asking about our summer plans, but I couldn't
hear her. "*I have five kids!*" my brain began screaming at me. "*I have five
kids! They may not all be home for the summer, but I have five kids!*"

The orthodontist was looking at me expectantly again, but I didn't
know why. She repeated some inane question about our summer plans as
this idea continued to scream in my head. I answered as blithely as I could,
not sure how to silence the chaos. I felt like I needed to tell her about
Russell, to let her know that I indeed had five kids, but I just didn't know
how. I was already close to a breakdown. My children would be mortified
if I burst into tears in the orthodontist's office with other people looking
on.

Didn't the office staff remember that Russell had come with us to all
of the appointments before he died? How could they not know I had five
children and that one of them was conspicuously missing?

In the end, I chickened out, and I felt like I'd let Russell down, like I
had betrayed his existence. After we got home, I told the children I was sick,
and I went to bed, even though it was midafternoon. I was inconsolable; I
couldn't cope. I lay on my bed and sobbed. Miserable. Destitute. I felt like
my insides were being torn apart, ripped to shreds from the excruciating
emotional pain. It hurt worse than anything I could imagine, and I couldn't
stop crying. I couldn't control myself. Finally, I just gave in, letting the hurt
and pain tear at my insides and rip me apart because maybe the tears would
end then. They just kept coming.

After a few hours, I went downstairs and made some spaghetti for the
kids. It was starting to get dark, and I told them to come inside. I showed
them what was for dinner and went back upstairs. The torrent of tears
reappeared, along with harrowing pain. I writhed and struggled because
of the severity. I needed to include Russell when people asked about the
number of my children, no matter how painful it would be for me to say
that I had lost him.

* * *

Summer was now past, and the children were getting ready to return to school. Russell had been looking forward to kindergarten. He'd been ready and excited for it. He'd died nine months before that important milestone in his life.

We went to the school the day before classes started to see which classes and teachers everyone got. This had been a fun tradition, usually followed by a Slurpee or other yummy treat. I didn't want to go this year; we wouldn't be looking for Russell's kindergarten teacher. Depression set in; everything seemed to be a sharp reminder that my little boy wasn't there. I had survived the summer, but as we rounded this corner, I saw too many empty days ahead. The children would be going back to school.

How would I fill the time? Joey was my only one left at home, and he was anxious for me to set up playdates with his friends. After school started, I had Halloween, Thanksgiving, Christmas, and finally the first anniversary of Russell's death looming in the near future. Checking the class lists that afternoon wouldn't be just one bad day for me; it would be the start of a bad season.

I went to the school after all, and after finding out whose class each child was in and comparing their teachers with all of their friends' teachers, we headed over to the playground. So many families were at the school, each pushing and smooshing to get a good look at the lists. I felt claustrophobic and couldn't get away from the crowd of people fast enough.

People stared at me and then looked away as our eyes met. I'm sure they were wondering if they should say anything. Or maybe they were wondering *what* they should say. It's hard to know if it would have been more helpful had they said hello. Engaging in idle chatter would have made me feel worse, like Russell had already been forgotten. But if everyone said something about him, I would have felt bombarded. Perhaps a simple "I'm thinking about you" kind of message would have been safe enough for them to say and for me to hear.

In the end, I only spoke to a few good friends, and that was almost too much. They were kind enough to acknowledge that Russell would have been in kindergarten. That recognition validated my rocky emotions.

We went to the playground and ran into a friend. She lived in my neighborhood, and for a time we had been in the dinner group together. She had three children the same ages as three of my kids. I hadn't seen her for a while; the dinner group had disbanded a few months after Russell's death.

She asked about the teachers my children had. I politely asked about hers. She had a kindergartener that year and asked if I had a kindergartener too.

The question took me off guard, and I answered with a gruff, "No."

"Really?" was her response. "I could have sworn you had a kindergartener this year."

How could I answer that? Surprised that she would remember I had a child her child's age but not remember that my child had died, I blinked away tears that she somehow couldn't see and just shook my head. *I used to have a child your child's age*, I wanted to say. *I was supposed to have a kindergartener this year*. It would have been too awkward a conversation, and I didn't trust myself to say the words kindly or without too much emotion attached. I couldn't bring myself to gently remind her that I had lost my child. We watched her kindergartener innocently playing on the monkey bars, and I wondered if Russell would have done the same too if he were there.

* * *

September rolled into October. I had barely made it through the start of the school year and was anticipating quite a few worse days ahead. We would be going up to Utah for Thanksgiving, and I was terrified of revisiting all the places Russell had been on our last trip. It couldn't be avoided. Reminders of him would be everywhere.

I had learned by now that the first time through any experience was the hardest. But after the first time, I felt prepared for the next. I knew what to expect and how to steel myself for it. The fear of the unknown and the negative expectation it caused sometimes made the anticipation of the event worse than the event itself. Sometimes. I didn't want to take any chances with Thanksgiving.

I didn't want Thanksgiving to be the first time I visited the accident site. I didn't want Thanksgiving to be the first time I drove past the mortuary. Or any other place we visited. I didn't want Thanksgiving to be the first time we went to John's house, where we had stayed on that fateful trip. I didn't want to experience this myriad of painful firsts with my children watching. I wanted to be strong for them, and my greatest fear was that I would be a wet, sloppy mess, unable to cope with the pain.

The answer was easy: Kirk and I would go to Utah before Thanksgiving. General conference was coming up, so we decided to visit then. I was excited to attend sessions at the Conference Center and combine this awful trip with something I could actually look forward to.

The tears started once we passed the Utah state line and only intensified as we drove on.

We got off the freeway in Provo and realized we were right by the mortuary. We made our way there and just sat in front of it. Neither of us felt like we needed to go in. Just seeing it was enough.

We drove by the MTC, remembering the fun we'd had there, Russell pointing up when asked where he wanted to serve a mission. Oh, the irony of him now serving there.

We stopped at Rock Canyon Park, parking at the top. We walked slowly down the hill, seeing images of Russell and the others sledding down. There was no snow this time, which helped lessen the power of these images.

I was carrying a heavy bag of heart rocks, a picture of Russell, and an action figure he would have liked. We made our way, hand in hand, up the other hill while Kirk told me about their last moments together. Then I told him of mine. We looked down to see the tree Kirk and Russell had hit. It seemed like it had just happened yesterday, yet it was an entire lifetime ago that Russell had died.

We circled the tree, wondering how it could have the audacity to still be standing so tall and proud after causing something so life changing and painful. Not a scratch, not a mark indicated that this spot had caused my life as it was to come to an end.

This was treacherous ground, and yet it was holy. It seemed wrong that this place was so . . . *ordinary*. It was a regular, everyday park with a regular everyday group of trees.

An adjacent group of trees had a flowery bush planted next to it. Karina told me someone had planted it there shortly after Russell's death, presumably in honor of him. But it was in the wrong place. Almost without thinking, I began to dig it up. It felt good to dig, to fight the earth and the roots. I transplanted the bush to the proper spot and lay the heart rocks all around it. I carefully placed Russell's picture in my new memorial and left the action figure sitting alongside it.

Kirk and I sat there for a long time. I felt better leaving a physical memorial for Russell, even though I knew it probably wouldn't be there in November when we came back. It was little, and it was pretty, but most importantly for me, it marked the place where my life had been changed forever.

General conference was amazing. It seemed that most of the talks were written for me. There were so many talks that year on enduring through affliction and remembering the great love our Heavenly Father has for us. I wish I could describe the thrill I felt when President Monson walked into the Conference Center and everyone stood. It was electric. The surge of power renewed me and filled me with emotions I hadn't felt in almost a year.

I felt like I had been traveling in the desert—hot, dusty, dying for hunger and thirst. Conference was like an oasis. I drank it up. It was a feast, and it filled me.

I was able to take this renewed strength back to California, and it helped get me through some of the worst days of the year that were to come. I know those upcoming days would have been more terrible and difficult to get through without the added concentration of the Spirit I received from general conference.

\* \* \*

Our first Halloween without Russell was coming up. I stayed away from department stores as much as I could so I wouldn't see the displays of Russell's favorite holiday. Of course, the magic of neighbors giving him candy for free was a big draw, but dressing up was what captivated him the most. He felt powerful in those costumes, able overcome the many childhood insecurities he had. He loved the looks he would get when we were out running errands. Everyone could see how strong and able he was. But to Russell, these costumes were his everyday wear. At Halloween, he needed a *new* costume, and he spent the entire month of October contemplating his choice. It was a big decision for him, one he took seriously. I couldn't stand looking at costumes now, but Joey always wanted to see them and dream about what he would be. Just walking through the aisles of superheroes and villains made me teary and sad. Sometimes I choked on my own breath, as if running out of air. Then I'd insist we hurry away—as far away as possible from the painful reminders that my little boy was gone.

The day of our ward's trunk-or-treat was the hardest of all. Russell would have been so excited to dress up and get all the candy he could. I moped around the house all day, finding no relief. My heart and lungs actually hurt with every tortured breath. My eyes stung with the tears that would not stop coming. I didn't even wipe them away because when Russell cried, he never wiped his. I just sat there, getting wet and more despondent than ever. I really wanted to talk to somebody, but I didn't know who to call or what to say.

I knew there were lots of people who would have wanted me to call—hadn't they all said, "If you need *anything*, even just to talk, call me"? But I felt embarrassed. I didn't know how to bring it up. I was self-conscious about my grief and clumsy in expressing it. It was unwieldy and cumbersome. It was difficult to maneuver; even the thought of laying it on someone else's lap seemed graceless and gawky. I didn't want to be alone in this, but I didn't know how to reach out.

If only someone else would have called and asked, *really asked*, how I was doing, maybe then I could have shared how deeply I hurt. But I felt pathetic and pitiful desperately searching for someone to talk to. Didn't anyone think that on *this day* I might be vulnerable, sad, and needing a friend? Didn't anyone think that on *this day* I might need a phone call?

I felt sorry for myself because the loss seemed so profound on this day. I allowed myself to wallow too deeply in the pool of self-pity. My heart and my conscience gave me permission to go as deep as I wanted.

Until I went in too far.

My thoughts became dark and loathsome. I pled with the Lord to send someone to help me, but no one came. In my selfishness, I began to feel abandoned. *If anyone* really *cared about me, they would call or come over*, I reasoned viciously.

Suddenly, I was rebuked by a sharp, reproving thought: *you* know *that's not true.*

It wasn't *my* thought, and in my mind, it didn't sound like my voice. The voice allowed me to feel sad, but it refused to let me cross the line into innuendoes and lies.

I was taken aback by this sudden rebuff and had to admit that my thoughts had been headed in the wrong direction. I had many friends. I had been lifted up and sheltered by them. They cared deeply for me and my family. They had proven themselves throughout this entire trial. My mind caught hold of all the good that had been done for me and my family in the last ten months. It raised my spirit. I felt the comfort of these friends—people who had given freely of their time, means, talents, thoughts, and prayers in an effort to strengthen and succor me.

My way of thinking changed as a result of an idea coming into my mind. Again, a thought that wasn't mine. I believe it was the voice of someone who had passed beyond the veil. I could get off my couch. I could change out of my sackcloth and ashes. I could see the good even while I was sad.

Kirk and I had previously "checked in" and explored our feelings toward the upcoming holidays. Trunk-or-treat didn't hold the same painful significance for Kirk as it did for me. He was excited to see all the different costumes and to pass out candy, and he was looking forward to taking the kids. Since he was happy to go, I felt I could stay behind.

While home alone, I got a special treat. A friend in the ward came over. For different but just as painful reasons, she didn't want to go to the trunk-or-treat. We sat and talked, me telling her of my sorrow and she telling me of hers. Our gloom turned to laughter and our wretchedness to peace as we shared our burdens.

I have always thought that "blessed are they that mourn: for they will be comforted"[15] made no sense. How could those who mourn be considered blessed? The blessing comes in the act of being comforted. I was comforted in many different ways on this awful day—one of my worst since Russell's passing. I was comforted in the memory of the gracious deeds performed by friends and family. I was comforted in the reproving voice that would not let me lie. I was comforted by the friend who ditched the trunk-or-treat with me. I think, though, that much as with giving the Russell rocks to others who were hurting, the greatest comfort came when I stopped thinking about my loss and recognized the loss of another. The most comfort came for me that day when I saw someone *else* mourning and I reached out to comfort her.

* * *

When we headed to Utah for Thanksgiving, I prayed and prayed for no snow. Thankfully, my prayers were answered. It was weird to see how much my nephew Isaac had grown and matured since the new year. Russell had been a good six months older than Isaac. They had been good friends and seemed to be growing at the same rate. If one spurted up, pretty soon the other one had a growth spurt to match. They had different personalities, but they usually had a great time together. Seeing Isaac without Russell was hard. I tried not to stare and imagine, but I did anyway—how tall would Russell have been? Would he have been writing his letters and learning how to spell too? Of course he would have.

I had to be careful about my reverie because I was already on the verge of crying, and a few times my staring and wondering pushed me over the edge.

Seeing the cousins playing together was difficult too. Too many times I had to leave the room or cry in the bathroom. I'm sure Russell was with his cousins, enjoying the fun. I wish I could have seen him. Again, I felt physical pain at Russell's absence when his cousins played. I found it hard to concentrate. Midconversation, my eyes were constantly drawn elsewhere—

to a drawing by Isaac with his name neatly printed on the bottom. To Isaac's kindergarten homework on the counter. To the boys wrestling in the middle of the room. Lots of little things around me added to the clutter of what-might-have-beens in my head.

One night all the adults got together at John's house to watch a movie. It was about a superhero who didn't remember his past and, as a result, didn't want to help anyone. I'd wanted to see it, and I enjoyed the film—until the end. The climax found the superhero—now actively trying to save the world—and a female superhero in an emergency room. They were becoming mortal and dying. Of course, the bad guys were coming to finish them off before they could be healed.

The scene had a lot of commotion—nurses and doctors everywhere, the beeping of machines. It was way too realistic for me and brought me back to the ER. I could hear the noises, see the scenes, feel the emotions and fears coming back to the surface. I could almost smell the iodine and feel the dread we felt as we watched the doctors performing CPR.

It was too much; I could barely breathe. I was having another panic attack. And it ramped up when one of the superhero's hearts stopped beating and the doctors began performing CPR on her. I wanted to leave the room, but if I did, everyone would follow me out to see if I was okay. I didn't want that. I wanted to be alone, to gain control of my breathing and emotions. The room got claustrophobic. I ached to look away from the movie, to put my hands over my ears and scream—anything to block out the hospital noises. If only I could turn myself off, get away from the images and sensations threatening my sanity.

But I couldn't do anything. I sat there, motionless, helpless, feeling assaulted on every side.

*I should do something*, I thought, but my mind was paralyzed and couldn't give me any information. I was trapped, sucked into a story I knew too well.

I was *in* that hospital room. It wasn't the superhero on the table; it was Russell. The images played out in front of me over and over again. Of course, the superhero came back to life, as I knew she would.

It wasn't fair! That wasn't how life really worked—that wasn't how it worked for me.

*I wanted her to die.*

I wanted her to stay motionless and slowly become cold as her organs stopped receiving warm blood. I wanted the other superhero to fall down in unbearable anguish, barely able to comprehend what was happening. I wanted time to stop or at least slow down while all of the actors wandered around, dazed and confused. I wanted them to bury her and live their lives in the very pain and torment I'd experienced without Russell.

But this was Hollywood. They don't have that kind of sadness there.

So, of course, the long, unending pitch of the heart machine began beeping again. Our heroine slowly regained color in her cheeks and movement in her limbs. Then her eyes fluttered open to the amazement and relief of everyone.

Except me. I was angry. How *dare* she be able to come back to life after her heart stopped beating? What made *her* so special that her life should be spared? After putting me through an emotional wringer—after making me relive the worst experience of my life again—how dare they continue their lives as if this were just another day?

As soon as the final credits rolled, I sprang from my seat and ran out into the hallway. Unfortunately, Grandma Hess was right behind me. I choked back tears while we made small talk about the movie. Kirk's sister came out next, looking for candy. I heard the others coming, and the panic started up again. I could *not* be around people right now. The walls seemed to be closing in; I needed to get away.

"I'm walking to Karina's," I mumbled as I ran up the stairs and out the door. Her house was only a few blocks away through a park, but it was late and cold.

I was halfway down the street, hiccupping loud sobs and gasping for air, before I realized Kirk's sister hadn't seemed surprised like she normally would be by my walking home. The air felt icy, and the grass crunched with frost under my feet. Walking home wasn't a big deal, but I had only a thin sweatshirt on, and she would have at least asked if I would be warm enough. The sick realization washed over me that she probably didn't understand what I had said and wouldn't have known that I had left.

But it was too late now. I was crying uncontrollably. Loud, rasping sobs shook my entire body. Hot tears streamed down my face. I could see my breath as I cried, but I couldn't feel the cold.

I made it to the park and sat there, watching the exit of John's neighborhood. I knew once I saw my sister-in-law's car leave I had about ten minutes before they would be home. I'd walk the shortcut through the park into her neighborhood while they'd have to drive all the way around on the streets. Even though I had planned my escape, my mind was focused on other things. I was being hurled into scene after scene of losing Russell.

I saw his eyes, unfocused and unseeing, as he lay lifeless on the emergency room table. I saw the doctors tirelessly working on him, even though, by then, I knew he was gone and had passed far beyond my reach. I felt the weight of his dead body as it grew colder and stiffer by the minute in my arms. I saw him in the coffin, pale and angelic, his skin so hard and cold.

Alone in the dark, in front of the swings and play equipment, I was on all fours, dry heaving on the frozen grass. I was in an open area, with no trees or bushes to hide behind. The park was surrounded by houses, yet at this moment, the thought of onlookers didn't compel me to rein in my emotions. I sobbed loudly, uncontrollably. I was back at the ER, being told the news, experiencing it all over again—only this time no numbness masked the pain. This time the ache and the emptiness and the horrifying pain of the last eleven months were also ripping me open and tearing me apart.

All over again, someone had reached into my heart and mercilessly pulled it out. I was sprawled out on the grass, shivering so hard I couldn't see straight. I wanted to die.

I wanted to *die*.

Not just to see Russell. If dying meant the absolute end of me, no resurrection to eternal life, just the complete snuffing out of my light—I would have welcomed it. In fact, I prayed for my complete annihilation.

I knew I had four living children and a loving husband who needed me alive. They needed me around, and I didn't want to leave them. But the torment at that moment seemed too much for me to bear.

I also knew God wouldn't let me die. Just as I had known in the hospital that it was Russell's time to go, I knew that now wasn't my time. I felt selfish and weak, unable to break free from my demons, and yet I desperately needed some respite.

I wanted to be extinguished, to be nothing, because then the searing pain would also be gone. My lungs were on fire. My chest felt as if there was a gaping hole where my heart belonged. My face stung with the night's cold.

Again, I relived scenes from the past year. I wished my brain would blow up. This was by far the lowest moment in my thirty-eight years.

I hadn't ever felt this bad, and that was part of the problem. I'd had good moments, good days, even good weeks during this year without Russell. I confidently thought I'd turned the corner and was out of the woods. But now I'd walked into a wall. My emotions were as skinned and bloody as the first time.

That's what made this night so much worse. That's why I wanted to die. I lay in the park, facedown on the cold ground.

*I can't do it again*, I thought. *I can't experience Russell's death again.* But I might have to. If I got through tonight—exhausted and empty—then what? I might be fine for a week or two, but another emotional breakdown was bound to be out there, lurking in the dark, around a blind corner.

I couldn't live like this, not emotionally, not mentally. Not physically. The pain became less about my need to see Russell and more about my need to be free from the nightmares that held me bound. I didn't know what to do, but something had to change.

I quietly tried to regain control. The others had seen this movie before. Why in the world would they suggest Kirk and I see a movie that took place in a hospital where someone's heart stopped beating? I knew they hadn't done this to be mean. They simply hadn't connected the movie with our experience.

Then it dawned on me: no one else but Kirk knew what had happened in that hospital room. No one else saw how the flurry of doctors and nurses trying to save Russell had dwindled to a single orderly cleaning up as quickly as he could while I held my cold, dead son. There was no noise, no chaos, no panic, no hope when family came in to say good-bye. No one else saw the violence—and CPR is a violent thing to watch, especially when it's your son they're performing it on. No one had any idea of my trauma because I had told no one. To keep the past from unmercifully repeating itself by mistake, I had to tell my story.

The car came out and drove slowly past the park, but then it turned around and headed back. I was puzzled at how long they'd taken and why they'd turned around but felt apathetic and in no condition to be heading back to my in-laws' house.

Realizing they might return any minute, I tried to regain my composure. I couldn't.

My enlightened moment did nothing to lighten my mood. The torment began all over again. I half sobbed, half gasped for breath. I was no longer at a park in the middle of Utah but in my own personal hell.

Again the car drove by, going slower around the park. Finally they saw me, stopped, and Kirk came running. I was right; his sister hadn't heard me say I was leaving. They had been spending all of that time looking for me, frantic because they couldn't find me anywhere, which was ironic since I'd stayed for the entire movie so I wouldn't cause a scene in the first place.

I don't know how long we sat there, Kirk holding me, stroking my hair, both of us crying. It seemed we stayed that way, quietly talking and crying, for a long time. I told Kirk of my fears and my pain, and he told me of his. I felt my burden lifted as I shared it with Kirk. Slowly, I began to breathe normally again. Fatigue set in. We looked at each other and decided it was time to go.

All eyes were on us as we finally entered Karina's house. No words were said, but hugs were given and understanding looks were exchanged as we all cried for our loss together. That quiet support gave me all I needed to know.

I was not alone in this. I would survive this. Another breakdown might very well be around the corner, but if I chose, I would not have to struggle through it alone.

* * *

In October 2007, just a couple of months before Russell died, California experienced an unusually high number of wildfires. We felt sorry for all of the people losing their homes and being displaced while we were safe and unaffected in Orange County.

One night on our way home from Grandma Hess's house after Sunday dinner, however, we realized we were more involved than we'd expected to be.

The Santiago fire had begun. Started by arson in two places on our local toll road, the fire now raged through farmland and wilderness then started claiming homes in our area. On the third day of the fire, we could see it from our house.

By this time, countless fires raged from Santa Barbara County to the US–Mexico border. Resources were spread thin. If the fire came closer, would there be any resources left to help us? Luckily, we didn't have to find out. The fire burned parallel to our home and continued on to the Cleveland National Forest, where it was eventually put out.

In all, fifteen hundred homes were destroyed and five hundred thousand acres had burned. The fires had forced one million people to evacuate their homes—the largest evacuation in US history.

We were breathing ash and could see the black, charred remains of the fire nearby. I decided to write about it in our family Christmas letter, just a few short weeks before Russell died:

Hello, family and friends,

From our window, we can see some of the devastation left from the Santiago fire last month. It is a sad reminder of the damage one person can inflict, whether intentional or not. Out of the ashes, however, we were blessed to see the healing power of a community: the firefighters' and their families' sacrifice of time and energy as the firemen saved our houses, the volunteers who gave shelter to the newly displaced and homeless, and the donations of food, prayers, clothing, and money from the rest of us. We have the promise that our scarred mountains will be beautiful and green once again. During this season, we think of the Christ child in the manger. He has also promised us "beauty for ashes" (Isaiah 61:3). Our scars are healed through His perfect life and atoning death. We will be grateful to Jesus Christ forever. May you find the peace of the season in your life all year long!

Less than two weeks later, Russell was dead. The peace of the season couldn't smooth the jagged edges of our flesh from having our hearts ripped out, but the atoning sacrifice of our beloved Savior could. Though we had injuries that would scar, leaving indelible marks on our lives, we knew we could be healed through Jesus Christ and by partaking in the beautiful plan that had been designed before death could destroy us.

That first year after Russell died, I struggled for the words to describe how I felt about my Heavenly Father and His Son, Jesus Christ. I knew people expected me to be bitter or angry. But instead of animosity, I felt a closeness and a gratitude I'd never experienced before. Sure, I'd always believed in the gospel of Jesus Christ. I had partaken of the Atonement constantly to gain forgiveness for my sins. I believed and trusted in the plan of salvation.

But until Russell died, I hadn't experienced how necessary and beautiful the plan and the Atonement really were. Before, they were a good idea—something I would need eventually. After what I went through, I needed them, and they became a part of me. They were real, and I felt like I was looking at them for the first time.

I became overwhelmed by the organization and planning, the love and concern of my Heavenly Father. He had the foresight to know how death would affect us. He knew how final and absolute it would all seem.

Yes, how final and absolute it *would* be if not for an infinite Atonement to bridge the gap created by death and sin. Our Heavenly Father knew the fundamental principles by which the gap could be bridged. He painstakingly created a detailed plan in the eons before our bodies came to be to prepare the way for us.

I was awed by the planning required before the creation of the earth and all of its inhabitants. I knew this doctrine and had always loved it, but I so desperately needed that knowledge—*now.*

In the Christmas letter following Russell's death, I wanted to share my newfound discovery, to share how we were surviving. I wanted everyone else to see the beauty I now saw. I wanted them to experience the hope and the joy of the gospel. I wanted them to taste it because it was delicious. Though I struggled with the words, this is what finally came out:

Dear family and friends,

I've been dreading writing this letter for about six months now. That's when I realized it would be another one of those yucky "firsts" I'd have to do since our sweet little four-year-old Russell died. How can I describe how this year has gone by too quickly? How can I express the deep pain and depression we have felt? How can I express the immense gratitude we feel for the love and support we have received from all of you this year? How can I explain how we have survived?

In last year's Christmas letter, I told about the ruthless fires that ravaged the national forest behind our home. While looking at the devastation, I was reminded that we are promised "beauty for ashes" (Isaiah 61:3). There is a line on the mountain, scarred and brown on one side, green and unscathed on the other, where the fire changed direction. That line seems to mirror, in a small way, how 2008 has gone for us. Our lives were green and lush before Russell died. This year, we've become scarred and barren, aching for our loss and hurting for one of the treasures in our family that has gone on ahead. This has been in many ways an excruciatingly painful year.

Although we feel we are sitting in ashes, we are overcome with the beauty we have been given this year. We have been overwhelmed by the kindness and support showered upon us. These gifts of time and love have strengthened us and lifted us when we were most down. We can't even begin to share our appreciation for your thoughts, prayers, and loving service to us.

This has been a hard year, but it has also been a special year. We have seen the hand of the Lord in our lives more prominently this year. Even in Russell's death, we were able to feel a closeness to our Heavenly Father and His incredible love for us. That day was horrible, and yet it was special—even sacred. We were in the presence of loved ones who had passed on, and we could feel the assurance that this was part of the plan our Father in Heaven has for us. Although this was a detail of the plan we didn't anticipate, we know the outcome of the plan will be even better than we can imagine—that we will be together with our family and loved ones forever after death.

Every day this year has been like Christmas and Easter. Not because of the fun anticipation of presents and gifts of the season, but because we have so often thought about our Savior, Jesus Christ. Not an hour goes by that we don't think of Russell. And now every time we think of Russell, we think of Jesus Christ. We remember how Jesus wept with Mary and Martha at the death of their brother. He didn't take away the sadness of their loss. Instead, He mourned with them and gave them something better. In giving Himself, Jesus gave them eternal life.

Jesus has wept with us too this year. While it doesn't take away the sadness, it gives us comfort and joy for the future when we will be together again. I was grateful for the Atonement of Jesus Christ before Russell died, but now I can't even express how much more it means to me. The scriptures are more alive, more vibrant. I understand more clearly this plan of our Heavenly Father. I see now that in many ways, my life was barren and lifeless before Russell died, and now it is lush and full of understanding. It has been an amazing year. One filled with exquisite pain and sadness but filled to overflowing with hope, gratitude, appreciation, and love.

"For as in Adam all die, even so in Christ shall all be made alive" (1 Corinthians 15:22). Because of a little baby born in a stable, we have found beauty in the ashes of our year. May the promise of the season bring you peace in 2009.

It was amazing to see the change in me in one short year because of a single, short-lived event. That burned line in the mountain behind our home, where the fire changed direction, was still there for a few years after this second Christmas letter was written. I saw it every time I drove into our neighborhood. I often think about how my life is different, how *I* am different. I vaguely remember my life before Russell died. When I think of my past now, I feel removed from it, as if I'm peeking like a voyeur into someone else's memories. I only know that I am a changed person, a different creature. I have been made new, and there are days I still look at myself as a stranger. I'm still changing and morphing and trying to decide who I am and who I want to be.

All I know for sure is the love I have for my family, my friends, my Father in Heaven, and my Savior. My understanding of the gospel and of the scriptures has deepened. My commitment to my Heavenly Father has been cemented through my trials. I have been expanded, stretched beyond my bounds. I will never again be that carefree person on the other side of the line, but I have learned through the death of my sweet child that I will have beauty again one day.

* * *

Sometime in December I began subconsciously counting down. *Last year at this time*, I would remember, *we were out Christmas shopping. Russell had twenty-one days to live, and we didn't even know.*

The not knowing just added salt to the wound. I could see us there, a complete family, blissfully unaware of what was just around the corner. I was so innocent. So *happy*. It was the joy that tortured me the most. I was so *happy* last year, and I would never be *that* happy again.

The closer we got to the first anniversary of Russell's death, the more anguish I felt. The memories were still so fresh, so vivid in my mind. It was like Russell was dying all over again. Only this time, I knew all the gory details and had the pain of a year's worth of grief as I relived it. These visions tormented and teased me. They haunted me all month long.

This time last year, Russell found the Legos I had hidden for Christmas.

This time last year, we went on our last family campout with Russell.

This time last year, we went to Utah for a fun family trip.

This time last year, Russell was alive.

We had some vague plans of how we would spend January 1, 2009. I wanted to sit in a dark room and cry all day. I bought some flowers for us to plant in "Russell's garden" by our front porch. Kirk wanted to finish our family slideshow of 2008. The children wanted to bike to the park. We knew we would end up at the cemetery at some point, but other than that, we had no plans.

I envisioned a reverent, contemplative kind of day. I knew I wouldn't be able to really sit and cry the whole time, but I had the unrealistic expectation of a somber, quiet kind of atmosphere in the house.

This time last year, we were at the MTC, and Russell was pointing up.

The children were not quiet or contemplative. In fact, they argued and fought incessantly all morning. They didn't want to plant flowers but enjoyed it once I dragged them outside. Back inside, however, they started fighting again. We were all at our wits' end with each other. Something had to change. I accepted that we would not be commemorating this day the way I wanted anyway and decided to take the children on their bike ride to the park.

This time last year, we were sledding at Rock Canyon Park.

Once outside, their dark mood lifted and everyone got along. My somber house must have put too much stress on them, made the emotions of the day too heavy to deal with. They needed to go where they could enjoy the day.

While we were at the park, I looked at my watch and a miracle occurred for me.

This time last year, Russell was dead.

I remembered the emotions that overwhelmed me when I heard the news. I remembered his face, his naked body on the operating table, the shock of knowledge that my little boy was gone. The bustle of the doctors trying in vain to revive him. I remembered holding Kirk's hand as I looked up to see where I thought Russell's spirit would be. And then I remembered no more.

This time last year was worse than this time this year.

And for me, that was enough to end the torture. Last year couldn't torment me anymore because *this time last year was worse than this time this year.* The countdown was finished, I could turn it off, I could come back to the present, and I could move forward.

I watched my children playing at the park and smiled. I had made it through the first year.

That night as we all snuggled close and watched the slideshows Kirk had made—one family slideshow for 2008 and one slideshow of our life together with Russell—a quiet thought floated down and landed in my heart.

*We* are *making it.*

# Chapter Fifteen
## POSTRAUMATIC STRESS

AFTER RUSSELL'S DEATH, I'D EXPECTED anxiety. I'd expected irrational fear to seize me and not let go. After what I'd been through, I'd expected to be afraid and apprehensive. I was not disappointed. As mentioned, my first panic attack hit the day after Russell died.

After the funeral, the day the children went back to school, nine-year-old Kyle decided he wanted to walk the half mile downhill from our house. The children walked to and from school together every day, but Kyle wanted to walk *right now* so he wouldn't be late for school. No one else was ready, so that meant walking alone.

Anxiety clutched my chest. What if he were kidnapped? What if he got hit by a car? But I had to let him go because I could tell his anxiety was telling him he couldn't be late, especially today, his first day back.

So I let him go. After dropping the other children off a few minutes later, I walked up to the playground and frantically scanned it for Kyle. I tried to look casual as I avoided the moms I knew. I think they were avoiding me too. Once I saw Kyle, I ran back to the safety of the car—breathing heavily, heart beating wildly with relief.

My problem was, I no longer had a good reference point. Russell had died when I thought he was safe. I used to have a pretty good idea of what was dangerous for my children and what was relatively harmless. Not being able to find my child at a playground would not have stressed me out. I'd simply stop talking to the other moms, stand up, and look behind some of the slides. I'd always found the children there.

After Russell's death, I found myself compulsively scanning the playground every few minutes to make sure I knew where my children were. If I couldn't find them immediately, my heart pounded, and I struggled to breathe. I would jump up, frantically searching, panicked at the possibilities. Possibilities that were endless. And *real*. And *possible*.

Every random thought, every possible scenario, brought terror to my soul.

What if? What if? What if?

I had no idea whether I was being irrational or not. My worst fears had already been realized; how was I to know if my moderate fears wouldn't also come to pass? My son had died while sledding; who was I to say another one wouldn't die while playing at the park? Or at school? Anything could happen; I knew that now. My innocence was gone, and with it went the ability to rationalize away my fears.

One cold, dark, misty morning a month or two after Russell had died, I was out running with Tania. We were halfway up a very long hill on a deserted street when I saw something up ahead that made me want to jump out of my skin. Barely visible in the distance, something lay awkwardly on the grass. The feet were visible, the head slumped over.

It was a dead child, lying lifeless on the grass before us. I was struck with terror. I began to panic; I frantically looked at Tania, who would surely be as horrified as I was. She was midsentence, continuing our conversation. She couldn't have missed the body; we were almost there. How could she *not* be reacting?

I looked at the child again, which was in clearer view now. We would reach it soon, and she had not so much as skipped a step.

What should I say? What should I do?

I wanted to yell, to ask why she was being so callous. Was I overreacting? Was my panic disproportionate to the situation of seeing a dead child lying on the grass? I didn't think so, but I began questioning myself. Maybe I couldn't assess situations properly.

As we approached, its form changed. What I'd thought were feet weren't. The "head" was only the top of a bag filled with leaves and grass. *It* was slumped over. This close, I couldn't see how I could have mistaken it for a child. But I'd been *convinced*. I stared at the bag the whole time we ran past it, waiting for it to morph back into my greatest nightmare.

Noticing my heavy breathing and labored running, Tania asked if I wanted to walk the rest of the way up the hill. I just wanted to get away from that apparition as quickly as I could, as if running away from a bag of leaves could get me farther from my fears.

This was not an isolated incident. It seemed I saw dead children everywhere. My brain played cruel tricks on me, trying to make sense of figures and shapes in the distance. Even the billboards on the freeway appeared to have pictures of dead children until I was close enough to see the true images.

I could only imagine the horrors inkblot pictures would hold for me if I had to look at them. The death of my child was so encompassing that death was all my brain would let me see.

I had already experienced a few panic attacks by this time. Panic's cold, bony fingers would reach in my chest and squeeze my heart without mercy. I was choking. I could not breathe. I felt as if I were having a heart attack.

The first time I had a panic attack, I recognized it for what it was from my sister's description of one she'd experienced the year before. Although I wasn't frightened, I still couldn't breathe. My chest rose and fell, but I heard myself gasping for air. Logically, air had to be getting in.

"I *am* breathing," I told myself over and over while I tried to concentrate on getting air in. When that didn't work, I started thinking about a quilt I could make. I figured out the size of the squares and planned the yardage I'd need. Slowly my breathing returned to normal.

After experiencing several attacks, I learned that I couldn't control when a panic attack would hit, but I could control the attack once it came. I could calm myself down. I could get through it.

After a while, I recognized the triggers; panic attacks seemed to hit when I was alone. Sirens, ambulances, and shows depicting hospital scenes—especially emergency rooms—had the potential to bring one on. Thinking about Russell or wallowing too much in my pain could start one too. I once talked with an older lady in the library three months after Russell died. She had thin, white, waxy-looking hands that were almost translucent—the same color Russell's hands had been after his spirit had left his body.

I couldn't stop looking at the librarian's dead-looking hands. I wanted to touch them, to see if they were as stone-cold as Russell's had been. I wanted to hold them and warm them. To breathe color back into them. I was held by a sick fascination, a morbid attraction to her hands. How could they look so dead when she was alive? I pulled myself away from the conversation as quickly as I could.

Then I had a panic attack. Apparently, dead-looking hands are also a trigger for me.

A year and a half after Russell died, my attacks began to lessen in intensity and duration. I assumed that as time passed, my panic would dissipate until it disappeared completely. Although my panic attacks became less frequent, they seemed to be replaced by anxiety attacks. During anxiety attacks, my chest tightened and I was seized with the fight-or-flight reflex. Nervous energy disrupted my apathetic lethargy.

The triggers for these new attacks were ridiculous. Being thirty minutes *early* for carpool pickup after school but worrying irrationally that I wouldn't get a parking spot. Going to the supermarket to get cereal and worrying that the one on sale was already gone. Always feeling like I had forgotten something important even though I had written everything down so I wouldn't.

Along with my increase in anxiety, I was more easily frustrated and always irritable. I was able to sleep, but nightmares still jolted me awake some nights. I have seen Russell's death replayed again and again behind sleeping and waking eyes. I have seen each of my children die in horrifying ways in my sleep, and each time was unpreventable. Waking from these terrors brought little peace, for at the back of my mind was always the possibility that they could happen in real life. I had experienced it once for real and was terrified of experiencing it again.

I was easily startled. I was extremely sensitive to noises—not helpful in our constantly loud house. I jumped at every little sound. My heart was constantly beating hard. I began to be on edge, unable to calm down.

I had a problem; I was suffering from post-traumatic stress disorder.

PTSD is a type of anxiety triggered by a traumatic event. Most people associate PTSD with war veterans who have lived through the grotesque and terrifying scenes of war. But anyone can develop PTSD after experiencing or witnessing an event that causes intense fear, helplessness, or horror.

People who have experienced or witnessed traumatic events often have a period of difficulty adjusting and coping. With time, the traumatic reactions usually get better. If the symptoms get worse or last for months or even years, this is an indication that PTSD has set in.

Symptoms of PTSD include intrusive memories such as flashbacks and dreams, avoidance of dealing with the trauma, anxiety and increased emotional arousal, irritability, trouble sleeping, and an increased startle reflex. I was a textbook case.

Friends encouraged me to see a therapist, but I considered *myself* to be my personal therapist. I was in tune with my emotions and constant fluctuations in moods and temperament. I'd come this far on my own; surely I could do the rest by myself.

I'm not against therapy or medication—I know it is helpful and even vital in many cases. But I was talking to myself more than I would have talked to someone else. I really felt I could work it out on my own. Besides, I'm pretty cheap, and I did not like the idea of paying someone else to fix something I could fix myself. I gave myself six months to see improvement. If I wasn't better by then, I could find a professional.

So I went to the library—avoiding, of course, the librarian with the "dead hands"—and got a book on PTSD. I read through it immediately. It was thoroughly interesting and gave me new insight on my issues.

But it didn't solve the problem. I still had anxiety. I could recognize it better now. I could determine whether my anxiety was rational or irrational, where it stemmed from, and how to calm it. I just couldn't seem to stop it from coming.

About this time our ward began our annual "read the Book of Mormon in ninety days" challenge. Every summer my bishop-husband encourages the ward, especially the youth, to read the entire Book of Mormon, six pages a day, from June to August. I'd tried the challenge the previous summer but couldn't concentrate long enough; the commitment seemed too overwhelming.

I still struggled to be consistent in my scripture reading. I listened to general conference on CD. I read meaningful verses and sometimes chapters of the Book of Mormon on my own, and I read a chapter a day with the children for our family scripture study. But it was time to take on the challenge and step up my studies.

I'd read and studied the Book of Mormon many times and was familiar with its stories. I had a strong testimony of it and had had many meaningful experiences with the Holy Ghost, received answers to prayer, and gained deep spiritual insights as a result of my reading in the past. I felt I knew the book inside and out; there wasn't much more for me to learn from it.

I couldn't have been more wrong.

Somehow, in my readings of the Book of Mormon, I'd missed its great message of dealing with loss. Now it seemed most of the prophets who wrote in it had struggled intimately with loss, whether it was the loss of a loved one or an entire people to sin or the loss of a loved one to death. I was taken aback at how comforting this inspired book was to someone who had lost a child. To me, every scripture now talked about the great plan of our Heavenly Father and the great love our Savior showed us by implementing that plan.

Even verses I was very familiar with took on new meaning as I read through the eyes of a bereaved mother. I was overcome not with grief but with the humble emotion of gratitude for my Elder Brother. I was consumed with both my nothingness and the great importance I held in my Father's eternal family. I cried with Amulek as he watched the believers being cast into the fire. I realized for the first time that his family might have very likely been among the victims. I marveled at his forgiveness of Zeezrom, whose poisoned remarks had led directly to the martyrdom. I was touched when Alma took in a disheartened Amulek and ministered unto him. I knew Amulek's type of bleak, suffocating pain. I cheered when Amulek had the strength to serve again and share the glorious message with others. I also knew that longing to bring the light that illuminated my soul into others' darkened lives.

I felt as Alma, who cried, "O that I were an angel. . . . Yea, I would declare unto every soul, as with the voice of thunder, repentance and the plan of redemption, that they should repent and come unto our God, *that there might not be more sorrow upon all the face of the earth.*"[16] I have shared the wonderful news of the Restoration and the beautiful promise of eternal families with my friends who have also lost children. I have been surprised and saddened at the lack of response. I have wished, as did Alma, that I could have had more power to convince them of the truth and the magnitude of this information.

I was surprised to read about how the Three Nephites were given the promise that they would "not have pain while . . . in the flesh, *neither sorrow save it be for the sins of the world.*"[17] I never wondered if it would be hard for the Three Nephites to say good-bye to their loved ones as they watched them grow old and die. Would their separation have caused a depression and apathy like mine? I knew now, of course, of sorrow's heavy hand and wondered if the Three Nephites would be effective missionaries of the Lord if they were sad and lonely without their friends and loved ones. I never considered how natural sorrow is. Everyone with a physical body experiences it.

I would think that Jesus had to physically change the three disciples so they would not feel this searing pain in losing their loved ones to death. Jesus promised the Three Nephites that this type of sorrow would be taken away from them and that only the sorrow for the sins of the world would have a place in their emotions. Reading this account made my own mortality more bearable. It helped me understand that the pain of grief and sorrow is a normal, natural byproduct of mortality. Grief is part of the process I am to go through, part of the plan.

Moroni made me weep. Alone, bereft, depressed, and discouraged, he wandered the land just waiting to die. His entire family had either been killed or had joined the evil band now trying to kill him. He had lost everything except his testimony and his resolve to choose the right. He saw no purpose, no reason to live. I'm sure he felt, as I have many times, how nice it would have been to die and be reunited with his loved ones. And yet he lived on. I'm sure he was confused and disheartened.

In desperation, he wrote from his heart. He finished the abridgement Mormon had started, then waited awhile longer. When it was apparent he would yet live, Moroni added his last words to the Book of Mormon and included special letters from his father, letters that are priceless to us. Did Moroni have any idea of how meaningful they would be to the readers of this inspired book?

I have felt like Moroni—staggering in pain after being bludgeoned by such devastating loss. I have wanted to die but have also realized that it isn't my time to go. While I won't be making as much of an impact on the world as Moroni, I will continue on, doing what I can. I'm attempting to live true to my testimony of Jesus Christ and His eternal gospel.

None of these stories was new to me, but now they *were* new because I was reading them differently. I had been there. Heck, I still *was* there! And now I learned that my friends in the scriptures had been there too. We walked our road together, strengthened by our common loss.

About a month into the challenge, I realized I felt more peace. I had more internal strength to buffer me from the fiery darts thrown at me by the adversary. And I hadn't had an anxiety attack for weeks. I didn't jump at every little noise anymore. I was less agitated and grumpy, more calm. It wasn't the book on PTSD that was healing me; it was the Book of Mormon.

In a conference talk, President Packer talked about how we would be able to change destructive or negative behaviors more quickly and easily by studying the doctrines of the gospel than by studying the reasons for the behavior.[18] I didn't really understand what he meant the first time I heard it. But I understood it after all that had happened to me. The Savior was able to heal my anxieties and soothe my stresses in a way that I could not. The truths and the lessons in His holy scriptures are the balm to calm the troubled soul. Where I was helpless to help myself, my Savior and my Father in Heaven were able to help me—once I let them. Once I reached out and opened the scriptures.

# *Chapter Sixteen*
## MIND OVER MATTER

ONE SUNDAY, ABOUT A YEAR and a half after Russell died, Kyle stayed home from church with the flu. I made him a bed on the couch; put the phone, some crackers, and a bucket all within reach; and said good-bye. Kyle weakly said good-bye as he rolled over to go to sleep.

On the way home three hours later, Jake asked, "What if Kyle died while we were at church?" I looked in Jake's big worried eyes and answered, "Then we will be very sad. But we will trust in God and stay strong so we can be with him again."

It was surprising to me that my answer for Jake came so easily. It was surprising that *that* was the answer I gave. Actually, I had been thinking the same thing. What if Kyle *had* died while we were gone? I worried what I might find when we got home. My answer for Jake was the same thing I'd been telling myself for three hours.

I like to be prepared, to know how to react in any given situation. I don't like surprises, especially now—because I'm afraid something bad and unexpected will come out of my mouth or I'll do something I'll regret. I try to anticipate, to be prepared, but everything I face is so new.

When Russell died, I'd told Kirk it was not his fault, and I meant it. Secretly though, I was afraid of how I might react to future situations where I had to rely on Kirk. Would I be less likely to trust him? Would I inadvertently say something when he was with the children that implied I didn't trust him? I felt I did trust him, but I worried that since I felt so panicked and anxiety ridden I might do or say something to cause hurt and create a distance between us.

I got the answer on our first road trip, the one to Death Valley. Our first full day was spent on the sand dunes next to our campsite. Kirk, Kyle, and Jake wanted to check out the higher hills that were farther away. Joey wouldn't get into the child backpack, so I stayed with him, and Karissa kept us company. It was hard to always tell where the boys were. They'd go up a ridge then disappear on the other side. Then I'd see them on a higher ridge only to lose sight of them again.

Karissa was worried after the boys had been gone awhile. I wasn't worried, though, and I told her that they were safe because they were with Dad. I told her I trusted Dad and that he was a great father who knew how to keep his children safe.

It wasn't until later that night when I was alone in our van with a sleepy Joey that I reflected on our conversation. While I sat in the quiet and Joey dozed, I realized that I really *did* trust Kirk, and I realized again how grateful I was that Kirk was with Russell when he was called home. On the dunes, I had no misgivings or second thoughts about Kirk taking the boys off alone—no unfounded worries, no secret fears. My knee-jerk reaction to Karissa's concerns had been to trust Kirk. I was able to have a sweet conversation with my Heavenly Father in the quiet of the car, and I felt an overwhelming sensation of love and concern from Him.

After our campout in Death Valley, when Kirk and I were preparing for our first trip without the kids, my friends gushed over how lucky we were. "Aren't you so exited?" they asked. "You are going to have so much fun!" they exclaimed.

But I was afraid, gripped with worry. What if one of my children died while we were gone? Could I go through it all again? Could I forgive my parents or whoever else was in charge of them? How could I ever survive?

I decided that I *would* survive. That I would be able to forgive. That I would be given the strength I needed. That Heavenly Father would help me the same way He'd helped me so far.

I repeated these thoughts over and over until the answer became my standard response when my fears and worries threatened to overtake me. So when Jake asked me on that quiet Sunday, "What if Kyle died while we were gone?" I was able to tell him that I had also had that same thought. Then I was able to bear testimony of the goodness of God and my faith in Him no matter what.

The scriptures say that if we are prepared we shall not fear.[19] I feel I have mentally prepared myself as well as I can. I may still have worries, but I know that with God's help and as I exercise my faith in Him, I can have the peace that passeth understanding.[20]

## Chapter Seventeen
### SURPRISED BY JOY

I SEEMED TO REMEMBER MANY details about the time my neighbors' children died, many seemingly insignificant vignettes I don't consciously remember recording. One neighbor became almost obsessive with exercising, walking mile after mile on a treadmill in an attempt to get away from the pain. I'm sure she wasn't sleeping. She had a hard time putting thoughts and sentences together. Her pain was palpable, and just looking at her broke my heart.

She was losing weight but couldn't eat much. I worried about her health and wondered what to say to help her. Then she confided how some of her friends were trying to get her to eat because they were afraid she was becoming anorexic. I didn't think so. I saw that her unbearable grief, the loss of control, and her sorrow had simply made her incapable of eating. I decided not to nag her about food; she already had people doing that. Instead, whenever we talked, I tried to listen more. Over the months, she slowly made healthy changes.

Then Russell died, and she told me how she'd felt guilty after her son's death—guilty that *she* could eat. That she could breathe. That she was alive when her baby was not. When joyful moments snuck back into her life, she felt guilty being happy.

"You might feel the same way," she warned me. "Realize that you *can* be happy again—and one day it will be without guilt."

Mentally I knew this to be true. I had watched my sweet neighbor struggle for many years. I also knew Russell wouldn't mind me enjoying life, but he'd also understand me mourning his passing for as long as I needed.

I did have happy moments, times when I could smile and even laugh. But they were short-lived. I'm sure I fooled a lot of people into thinking I was fine or over it. But I was still so incredibly sad so much of the time.

I got to a point where I just accepted the fact that I would not be truly happy again until my family was once more complete. And I could live like that. I could accept that as my fate and still live righteously and well. This acceptance freed me from my search for an elusive happiness and allowed me to live more in the moment. It let me better enjoy those happy times when they came. This may sound like a bleak existence, and maybe it was to some degree—but I wasn't happy anyway, so my acceptance of this kind of life didn't make it any more bleak. Everything seemed blank and colorless with Russell gone.

By accepting my fate, I could laugh and enjoy my family and friends and my lot in life a little more. I simply stopped reaching for the level of happiness I'd experienced while Russell was still alive. I stopped comparing where I was now with where I had been before.

One day, while driving the children somewhere, I suddenly felt *good*. But something felt wrong with my face. The muscles on one side felt odd and strangely abnormal—like they were being pulled in an awkward position. I remember being worried that I was having a stroke. Frantically, I looked at my reflection in the rearview mirror.

And found myself smiling. For the first time in many months, my lips had turned up in a natural reaction to my mood. It had been so long since I'd smiled, really smiled, that my cheek muscles actually hurt from the strain as they remembered what to do in response to my joy.

* * *

One place I looked for happiness was in my quilting. But the promise of a new quilt brought me little joy after Russell's death. Where quilting before had been an exciting process, now it was painstaking work—almost drudgery. I persisted because I knew, in time, the magic would come back. As I mentioned before, I made many memory quilts that first year after Russell's death for new friends who had also lost loved ones.

Most were tied because hand quilting them took too long. I'd attempted machine quilting but never really got the hang of it. Then a friend bought a long-arm quilting machine and invited me over to try it.

A strange, vaguely familiar sensation flooded my chest. It was so different from the grief and panic I was used to. It took me a while to recognize what it was: anticipation. I was actually looking forward to something! An excitement bubbled effervescently in my spirit. Hope whispered into my heart that maybe I could be happy again.

* * *

When working on the Russell book, I put off writing about the accident. I just wasn't ready. So I wrote *around* the accident until I could avoid it no longer. I suppose I could have excluded it from Russell's biography, but that part of the story needed to be told. I wanted to include it; I just didn't want to revisit it. I wasn't ready to return to all the emotions waiting for me when I was still so overwhelmed with the ones bombarding me every day.

But I knew I had to. For two weeks I spent as much time as I could handle writing. I didn't spend a lot of concentrated time—just a few hours here and there around my kids' schedules. I didn't want to write about it when they were around because I became so immersed with the book; it absorbed me, transporting me back to a beautifully sacred yet soul-wrenching place that had threatened to destroy my very being. I had a hard time decompressing after those trips through time. Being alone was a must.

After the children went to bed one night, I determined to finish writing about the accident. When I did, it was almost midnight. I dragged myself, bleary-eyed, to bed. As I lay there, a warm glow engulfed me.

Yes. I finally felt peace.

I felt the satisfaction of a job well done, a job that Russell and the rest of my Heavenly Family were proud of. I realized, as I lay there, that I was proud too. I was surviving. What I thought might never happen again was gradually happening, and I was surprised. Surprised by joy.

# Chapter Eighteen
## THE DEBT

As WE WERE APPROACHING THE first anniversary of Russell's death, I found myself often in deep introspection. I contemplated what I'd endured over the last year, what I'd learned. I reviewed the incredible love and support of family, friends, and even strangers. I saw how my testimony of and love for the Savior had grown and deepened. I held a new admiration for the Atonement and had a greater appreciation and reverence for it.

I saw the changes in me, changes and growth that could not have come any other way. I was different now. I had new eyes.

But one thing about me that hadn't changed was how I felt about debt. I had been taught to avoid it like the plague. Kirk and I rarely make an expensive purchase, and if we do, we plan it out, budget for it, and pay it off as quickly as we can. We've always lived within our means and are lucky that both of us are not extravagant in our tastes.

One day almost a year after Russell died, I was out running with Joey in the stroller, thinking again of all the things that had been done for me and my family in the last year.

*I can never repay it all.*

The thought hit me suddenly. Not in a million years. If I "paid it forward" for the rest of my life, I still wouldn't begin to touch all the love, support, food, money, prayers, fasts, kind words, and more given to us. These acts of service meant so much to me and were so necessary for my survival during that painful first year.

These gifts—freely given with no expectation of repayment, only the hope of bringing us peace—were what initially helped us through the crashing waves of pain. They gave us strength when life became unbearable. They gave us joy when life became meaningless. They gave us peace when anxiety and fear weighed us down. They buoyed us up when we couldn't stand on our own. In short, they saved our very souls from being dragged down to an unbearable hell.

How can you repay that?

The sudden realization stopped me cold. I stood there with the stroller, trying to wrap my brain around a debt so large and freely given that I would be indebted forever. It was a beautiful yet horrifying realization.

I started running again, and another, more startling, more overpowering realization formed: *this is how the Atonement is.* This is *what* the Atonement is. I can't earn it, no matter how much good I do. I can't "deserve" it by my righteousness. And I can never, ever, even throughout the eternities, pay it back. It is a gift freely given by a loving Elder Brother in the hope that we will partake of it, in the hope that we will want to qualify for it and enjoy it.

The extent of my debt to my Savior is unfathomable. Unchartable. Incalculable. No matter *what* I do, I am still saved by grace.

I knew there were things I could do that would help me realize a brighter domain in the kingdom of heaven, but right then, that's all they were—just things. I was entirely overcome with the thought of my utter dependence on the Atonement of Jesus Christ. He'd snatched me and my family from the jaws of death, saved us from endless suffering.

Christ's Atonement—so willingly given—had saved my little boy from eternal torment and from simply being "snuffed out" or extinguished. Because Christ died for us—because He died for *me*—I'd have the opportunity to see my dear, sweet child again. I would be able to hold him again, to love him, to raise him, to cherish him.

I had never considered this part of the plan of salvation. Triumph over death is the *free* gift of the Atonement. The one everyone qualifies for. The one we don't have to earn.

Triumph over sin requires work. It requires repentance and forgiveness. Something given on our part. Because of the—dare I say it?—*inexpensiveness* of the Resurrection, I'd always taken it for granted. It hadn't cost me anything, so I assumed its worth was not as great as the more expensive gift of forgiveness. But now I desperately needed the gift of the Resurrection. I was lost without it. Now I saw its worth and realized my inability to ever repay it. Jesus Christ gave even when it was not appreciated, and that made my debt feel even more enormous.

Never had I so pondered my total reliance on my Savior. He was eager to save me! I'd never felt so small, so helpless, or my deeds so insignificant. Yet I never felt more loved or important.

Through the selfless service and unflinching love of my friends and family, I gained a deeper, stronger sense of the Atonement. I was able to see, through my debt to them because of their gifts to me, how indebted I was to my Savior. And through my vast debt to the Lord, I felt my immense worth.

## Chapter Nineteen
### WHY

WHEN I WAS A TEENAGER, my family went to a family counselor. We had problems relating to each other and weren't communicating well. My parents felt they'd lost their parental control over us and that the inmates were taking over the asylum.

They were right. I was a pretty ornery teenager and knew pretty well how to work the system. My older brother and I took full advantage of our parents' busy lives and lack of follow-through. We pushed as hard as we could, then pushed a little more to see what would give. With five younger children coming up in the ranks after us and learning the ropes, my parents became desperate.

Our therapist assured my parents he could help them get "back in control." He had proven methods that would help them to assert their dominance and pummel us into submission. At least, that's how we children interpreted it. We were *not* on board.

He gave my parents index cards with the words *regardless*, *nevertheless*, and *irregardless* printed on them. He instructed my parents to hang these cards all over the house and to use these nonsense words to quell fights and arguments when they had already laid down the law. It was frustrating as a teenager to be told, "*Regardless* of what you say, the answer is still no," especially after I had carefully prepared my case as to why the decision should be overturned.

While I did not enjoy the process, I did learn something valuable. After Russell died and I wanted answers from God, the same principle came to mind. While it didn't give me the answers I was searching for, it gave me insight as to why I would not be receiving the answers I wanted.

When someone asks "why" to anything, they are usually asking for one of two things: either they really want to know the answer, or they are looking for points that they can discredit to change the answer.

For example, in school a student may ask, "When am I ever going to use this math?" The teacher may respond that knowing how to compare fractions will help the student in comparing prices at the grocery store. For one student, that answer may be enough. But the student looking to argue a point might say, "Well, I won't be the one doing the shopping when I grow up, so I don't need to learn this."

Sometimes the question is the same but the type of information the person is seeking is different.

I have found this to be true in all aspects of life, and sometimes I find myself questioning my motives. Am I truly looking for answers? Not always. Sometimes I find myself rebutting the answers. That's when I know my true motive is to *change* the answers.

We already know the answer to "why?"

That answer is simply "because."

When my children ask "why?" they usually want to change the answer. When I say, "Because," I'm either tired of answering the never-ending barrage of questions or I'm hoping that they'll simply trust my many, many years of experience.

When Russell died, I just couldn't ask, "Why me?"

That question seemed to imply, "Why not someone else?" In knowing the pain of losing a child, I could not give the same grief to *anyone*. I could not ask another to carry this heavy burden I'd been asked to bear. It was too extreme, too intense, too exquisite.

I could have asked, "Why?"

But I already knew why: it was Russell's time. It was part of our plan, and Heavenly Father could have and would have changed it if it wasn't time for Russell to return to his heavenly home. Quite simply, I knew the answer was "because," so I tried not to ask.

Even so, I found myself looking for another answer. Hundreds of people, touched by Russell's story, came to the funeral. We used this experience as best we could as a missionary tool to share the truths of the restored gospel of Jesus Christ and to talk about the plan of salvation. I had many personal and meaningful conversations with close friends. I shared my beliefs with them in ways I had never been able to before. And this time, they were open; they were receptive; they were interested.

I thought, *Maybe* this *is why Russell died.*

But then I had other experiences and thought, *Okay, maybe* this *is why Russell died.*

Truth be told, there is no one, solid, satisfying reason why Russell died. There are thousands, maybe millions of little reasons, little lessons learned as a result of his death.

If I look hard enough, I find reasons everywhere. But sometimes these "reasons" aren't good enough—not good enough for *my* child to have died. I want to argue that these lessons could have been learned in other ways, that Russell's death was unnecessary—too heavy a price—for this plan to still have been worth it.

Yes, lives have been changed as a result of my son's passing. That cannot be argued. But did he *need* to die for these changes to ultimately occur? Are there any reasons worthy of my son's life? And my loss?

That is why the answer is simply "because." Heavenly Father knows the answer. He knows the reasons, and He is asking me to trust His fatherly expertise. He is asking me to have faith in His eternal experience. Accepting "because" means accepting the Father's will.

I had never imagined Jesus wrestling with a "why" question and moving ahead on sheer faith because He didn't have all of the answers. But my eyes were opened when Elder Jeffrey R. Holland gave a moving talk in the April 2009 general conference.[21] He told of Christ's despair at being left completely alone on the cross. Our Savior knew that His disciples would not be with Him at the end as He fulfilled His eternal purpose. During the last supper, Jesus explained to them, "Behold, the hour cometh, yea, is now come, that ye shall be scattered, every man to his own, and shall leave me alone: and yet I am not alone, *because the Father is with me.*"[22]

Christ knew He could do all things with the Father beside Him, no matter how exquisite, how excruciating, or how bitter.

But later on the cross, Christ cried in agony, "My God, my God, why hast *thou* forsaken me?" as the Father temporarily withdrew Himself from the scene.[23] Apparently Christ had not fully comprehended the fact that He would have to complete the Atonement without the comfort and the support of His Father's spirit. Not knowing why and moving forward on faith alone is a mortal experience that even our Savior needed to struggle through. It wasn't easy, but He accepted the Father's will so He could finish the work He came to earth to accomplish.

In his book *The Infinite Atonement*, Elder Tad R. Callister writes that "this was a crisis hour of ultimate faith." In speaking of that critical moment and the Savior's need for faith, he quotes Elder Erastus Snow:

At length the time came when the Father said, you must succumb, you must be made the offering. And at this dark hour the power of the Father withdrew itself measurably from Him. . . . And when He was led to exclaim His last agony upon the cross, My God, my God, why hast Thou forsaken me? the Father did not deign to answer; the time had not yet come to explain it and tell Him. But after a little, when he passed the ordeal, made the sacrifice, and by the power of God was raised from the dead, then all was clear, all was explained and comprehended fully. [24]

I had always felt the companionship and empathy of the Savior throughout my ordeal. I knew that He intimately knew of my loss. That He knew my sorrows and uncertainties. That He understood my desire to know why.

But I never put it together that it was His experience on the cross—when His query went unanswered—that led to His empathy for me. I am grateful beyond measure that Christ was willing to descend below all so He could succor *me* through all.

So I have stopped asking why. I am trying to be still and know that He is God. I'm trying to live the best I can and to share as often as I can the lessons I've learned through this experience. I want every positive thing that can come from Russell's death to come. This is the best way I know how to show my Heavenly Father that I *do* trust Him and His plan and that I will follow it. This is not "blind obedience" because this trust was forged through the crucible of pain. I may not understand the "why" behind my experiences, but this I know: my Heavenly Father has never let me down, and I know He never will. I feel as Nephi when he penned, "And I said unto him: I know that he [Heavenly Father] loveth his children; nevertheless, I do not know the meaning of all things."[25]

Besides, searching for the answer to life's "whys" is exhausting. Usually we find no satisfying answers to make up for the crushing loss, loneliness, or the excruciating pain. To continually ask "why" sows seeds of discontent in one's soul.

Knowing why will not bring Russell back to me in this life.

"Trust in the Lord with all thine heart; and lean not unto thine own understanding. In all thy ways acknowledge him, and he shall direct thy paths."[26] I have found it's more productive and nourishing to my soul when I accept "because" as the answer and continue to move forward.

## Chapter Twenty
### ENOUGH

THOSE FIRST FEW MONTHS, I was so emotionally bereft that I was hardly able to respond to situations at all. I was in a constant fog, struggling to follow conversations or even a train of thought. It felt like slogging thigh deep through a swamp. Every movement took extreme effort, effort I did not have, and so responding well moved down my list of importance—often I just didn't even care. I was more concerned with just surviving. I was emotionally and physically unable to do better. If I were to go back in time with the sole purpose of fixing those "mistakes," I would still be unable to do better because I did the best I could at the time.

I slowed down, not taking on more than I could handle. I simply couldn't do most things anymore. People were reticent to ask me for favors, so my "slowing down" was less my doing and more an effect of my circumstances. I didn't feel guilt over slowing down. Letting people help me out only filled me with gratitude for their generosity. I did not feel less worth because I was unable to provide for myself or my family; I did what I absolutely *had* to do. And that was enough.

My children suffered terribly. No matter how hard I tried, I could not give them all of the emotional support they needed. But I did give them all I had, and I hope in the end it'll have been enough.

We made sure Russell was still a part of our family. We put up the pictures we had framed of him for the funeral. We prayed for him just like we prayed for the rest of the kids. We reminisced openly when memories popped into our heads. As I wrote Russell's biography, I shared the stories I was writing about.

Since I *had* to cry, and my older children found my constant tears to be disturbing, I tried to cry only when they were in school. Giving myself that time—time to be lost in my despair—was helpful, and I was usually able to pull myself together and have more control over my emotions by the time the children came home.

I say *usually* because some days the tears wouldn't stop.

The children quickly learned that if I disappeared into the garage or backyard that I was either on a particularly emotional phone call or needed time to compose myself.

As I've mentioned, I was constantly in fear because of my new perception of danger. I tried not to hold my children back because of my sometimes irrational fears. I tried to keep the worries inside and allow my children to be kids. At times I failed, and I became the overprotective mother hen, shielding them from my imaginary monsters. They could have rebelled or chafed under my thumb, but they didn't. Instead, they argued incessantly, as children will do, but in the end they usually succumbed to my authority.

Although they were generous with their expectations of me, my children still *had* expectations about what life should be like. They did not tiptoe around but let me know when I had to step up. They acted like kids, playing one minute and fighting the next. From reading child psychology books, I recognized this as healthy behavior after a traumatic loss. In many ways my children were back to normal. They were boisterous, fun loving, downright silly, and teasing.

At times I wished their grief were more like mine so that I could have some peace and quiet. But I also wanted them to get through this soundly and to have happy memories of this time and not to have residual problems as a result of doing it another way.

The child psychology books on helping children live through a traumatic loss warned me what to be wary of with my older three children. I could educate their teachers on what to watch out for. I felt confident that I was doing all in my power to help them strengthen their testimonies and their relationship with their Heavenly Father. I felt confident that they would be fine, that this was a difficult experience but also a defining moment in their lives. And that was enough.

But I didn't know how to help Joey. Here, my books were worthless. They said children under the age of three did not have the words or the understanding to deal with loss. The books gave no pointers, no suggestions of how to help. I could barely grasp the concept of death myself—how could I verbalize it and explain it to a child who was one year old? Joey had a few words under his belt and could understand a lot of things, but he couldn't understand why his playmate and best friend had disappeared and abandoned him.

And that's where I made some of my biggest mistakes.

As I mentioned before, Joey helped keep me going. I got out of bed every morning, made breakfast for the kids, and got them off to school. If not for Joey, I would have gone back to bed for the rest of the day. But there he was, as sad and needy as I was. He was helpless and terrified that I too might disappear. So we spent our days together, usually with Joey on my lap in a tear-filled snuggle. Joey followed me around the house, making sure I stuck around. We read many books and had many "conversations." He still napped during the day, so I got my "Russell time" then.

A little while after Russell died, Joey and I drove past the cemetery. On a whim, I pulled in. Joey noticed the detour and asked where we were going.

"We're going to see Russell," I said before my brain had a chance to register how that would sound to a one-year-old. I looked in the rearview mirror and cringed at seeing Joey's reaction.

He sat bolt upright in his car seat, excitedly looking out the window, craning his neck for a better view. "We see Russell?" he asked eagerly, as if it were too good to be true. Unfortunately Joey didn't realize it *was* too good to be true. "Russell here? Where Russell? Where Russell?"

Lamely I backpedaled, trying awkwardly to explain that we wouldn't be seeing *Russell*, just the place where he was left in the ground. We pulled up in front of the plot. Joey was still looking around in excited anticipation of seeing his brother again. Then he realized where we were.

"Oh, Mom," he began, exasperated and with bitter disappointment. "Russell not *here*! He up in the sky!"

I couldn't have agreed more. We drove away in silence and sadness from the place where Russell's spirit wasn't, wishing only that we could see the place where it was.

I was at a loss over how to explain it all to Joey, and he seemed to be struggling through his own turmoil. When walking past pictures of Russell one day, Joey pointed and said, "Russell." He looked at those pictures with wonder in his face. Another day, Joey tried to throw something at the pictures while screaming, "No, Russell!" I knew he was mad at his best friend for leaving without an explanation.

Some days I was mad too. What could I say? How could I explain it so Joey's little mind could understand?

An acquaintance of mine lost her baby shortly after birth. She'd told her subsequent children that their older brother lived with Jesus. I liked that sentiment. To me, it was a simple explanation of where this child was.

And being "with Jesus" evoked happiness and safety in my mind. So one day, I told Joey that Russell was "with Jesus."

Joey seemed to accept this explanation. At least he didn't comment on it. But I wondered how much he really understood. I found out the next Sunday when we attempted to walk through the chapel doors. "No church!" screamed Joey, "No Jesus!"

My jaw hung open. Joey was *angry*. Livid. Inside the chapel, the entire congregation heard Joey scream, "I don't like Jesus!"

I flushed with embarrassment, but I was also surprised. How could Joey not like Jesus? He'd only heard nice things about Jesus at church—what could have made him so angry? Then it hit me—my worst mistake ever. In Joey's little mind, Jesus had taken Russell from us and made Russell live with Him. Joey was outraged that this Jesus would do such a thing and, in retaliation, decided he did not want to go to church.

I was floored. In my desperation for Joey to have some kind of closure or understanding of Russell's death, I had inadvertently misled Joey to believe that Jesus was a mean man who'd kidnapped his brother.

Joey might be the youngest person in history to decide to leave the Church. Luckily he was still very much a minor without a choice in the matter, so I still brought him, albeit kicking and screaming. Not wanting to add fuel to the fire, I did not mention the Savior in Joey's presence. I thought I would give it a rest and see if I could explain it better in a few months.

Well-meaning friends offered to watch Joey so I could be alone, but they didn't understand that I *couldn't* be alone right now. Just knowing Joey was upstairs asleep in his crib was a comfort. Being alone with my thoughts terrified me. Alone, I would let those thoughts take me to depths that were hard to return from. Having someone there kept the monsters at bay. Even if Joey wasn't next to me, just knowing he was in the house kept me from wallowing in my sadness. It helped me to feel safe. Joey was always there. I tried not to rely on him too much, and I tried to have friends over for him to play with so he would not become too reliant on me. We talked all the time. Or, I should say, *Joey* talked all the time.

By the time he was just over two, Joey was able to have short conversations. Then he'd ask, "Russell died?"

My emotions were still too raw to talk about it, so I would say, "Russell cried? Yes, Russell cried a lot when he was little."

"No!" Joey would interject. "Russell *died*."

"Russell sighed? Yes, I guess when Russell was sad then Russell would sigh."

"No!" an exasperated Joey would exclaim. "Russell *died*."

"Russell lied?" I would ask, feigning shock. "No, Russell did not lie."

At this point, Joey would growl in frustration, and I would deftly change the subject.

Instead, I should have been open and honest in helping him deal with his brother's death, but I physically and emotionally couldn't have that conversation. Joey tried though. He tried to broach the subject many times, but I danced around it, finding out just how many words there are in the English language that rhyme with *died*.

With time Joey grew more compliant in church. He still wasn't happy about being quiet during sacrament meeting, but he was getting better. I still didn't mention our friend Jesus more than I had to. One afternoon many months later, while I was organizing a bookshelf, Joey sat next to me, thumbing through books on the floor. I casually looked over to see what Joey was "reading." It was a picture book of the life of Christ. Joey was staring, in awe, at the picture of Christ on the cross.

He looked up at me. "Jesus died," he said in a reverential whisper.

"Yes," I answered. "Jesus died."

Joey nodded, and I could almost see the wheels turning in his brain. "Russell died." He said in a statement now.

I took a deep breath. "Yes," I began slowly. "Russell died."

A look of understanding crossed Joey's face. "Russell died. Jesus died." He spoke to himself as he began to work it out. "Russell died. Jesus died."

I tried to put it together for him. "Russell died and lives with Jesus because Jesus died too."

Joey nodded. "Russell died. Jesus died."

That was the most meaningful conversation we'd had about Russell's death. At that point, it was also one of the most meaningful conversations *I'd* had about Russell's death. Now Joey understood. Jesus was not some mean, heartless man who took loved ones away. Russell had gone to live with Jesus when he died because Jesus had died too.

Although I doubted whether Joey had a good grasp of what *death* was, he at least had a better understanding of who Jesus was. From that point on, I reintroduced Joey to Jesus. We read books about His life. We looked at pictures of Him.

Joey still does not like going to church. He fights getting his Sunday clothes on, but he has learned that it is not too hard to be quiet in sacrament meeting. More importantly, Joey has learned that Jesus is his friend. And for now, that is quite enough.

* * *

When Russell died, my extended family sprang into action. My parents notified all of my neighbors. They helped clean our house before we got home with my brother and his wife. My sister-in-law mentioned how vigorously my brother cleaned the toilets—how she had no idea he could be so industrious. They were there at the airport when we came home. They took down all of our Christmas decorations and put them away for us. My parents took our children to their house so Kirk and I could plan the funeral and make all of the arrangements.

My sister flew in from Texas and stayed with us for the funeral. Another sister flew in from Utah. My older brother gave her his frequent flyer miles so she could afford an airplane ticket. Storms raged on the East Coast, where two of my brothers lived. They both sat in different airports for days, trying to get on a flight to California. One brother succeeded, the other didn't. All in all, my family rallied around me, helping as much as they possibly could.

The night after the funeral, my mom and my sisters all sat together talking. We hadn't all been together in years. It was good to get caught up, to reminisce, and to laugh. It was healing to be together.

I have a close-knit family. We love each other, and we know we love each other. But we don't often *say* we love each other. In fact, we don't often say much to each other at all. We tend to get busy and don't make much of an effort to keep in touch. I'm as much at fault as anyone. We usually see each other once a year, though those of us in California see each other more often.

So I was surprised and touched to see the outpouring of love from my family in my time of need. I was succored and strengthened by them. It was a comfort to have them so close, so caring. After the funeral, though, everything went back to normal. My out-of-state sisters and brother flew home. My sister who lives an hour and a half away said, "Call me if you need anything." My brother who was living with my parents went back to his college life. My parents resumed their activities. My older brother who was unable to make it to the funeral turned around and went home. Only one person in my extended family thought to call me after the funeral to see how I was doing—my younger brother made it a point to call every few weeks for those first hellish months. He was the only one.

I was told by others who had lost loved ones to expect the attention to die down. They said after a few weeks or a few months the phone calls, the letters, the people checking up would lessen considerably as people moved on with their lives. That loss of support could cause another level of grief, I was told, but if I would expect it, maybe it wouldn't be so bad. I did expect it among my friends and ward members, but I didn't expect it from family. At least not so soon.

I was hurt. I was angry. I was depressed and tired. I knew that minimal contact was our family dynamic, but for some reason I imagined it would be a little different for at least a *little* while after Russell died. But no one seemed to care. We still went up to visit my parents, and my sister met us there with her kids. No one asked how I was doing. No one even mentioned Russell's name. It was like he'd never even existed.

My dad, who had spent years counseling people, mentioned the night of the funeral that I would probably have some kind of postraumatic stress because of Russell's death. He said he wanted to sit down with me later to talk about the signs and to teach me ways to combat it. He did once, over the phone, but it was not enough. I got the name of a therapist friend of his I could call to for insight. I really wanted to make sure my children were going to be okay, and I wanted to know what to watch for. The therapist called me back, and we had a brief conversation. She gave me some insight on healthy ways for my children to heal then asked how I was doing. She asked how my marriage was. She was surprised that I was not angry with Kirk, that I did not hold him responsible.

Her next comment to me was, "Wow. You sound like you are doing great." Then she hung up, evidently pleased I didn't need any more help.

But I was *not* doing great. I was sad. I was terrified that something would happen to one of my living kids. I was tormented in my dreams. I struggled during my waking hours. She just hadn't asked about those parts. Later, this therapist called my dad and told him her assessment. He assumed I was "cured" and never thought to ask me himself. When my parents called after that, it was to share inane information or to set up a family dinner. They never once asked how I was feeling, how I was surviving—*if* I was surviving.

I stopped pretending to be fine. I answered their questions with short, one-word answers. I got off the phone as soon as I could. When we visited, I didn't even try to smile. I barely made eye contact. I was acting petty and passive-aggressive. I was angry and didn't know how to tell them. I chose a childish and ineffective way to try to let them know. Only they didn't seem to notice my withdrawal. This made me more angry. I decided that if they didn't care, I didn't either.

The problem was, I *did*, and I knew that, deep down, they cared too.

I tried to let their seeming lack of interest go. I tried not to let it bother me. I failed. Not having my family's support agitated me. I had moments of fury

I couldn't get out of my system. Ironically, my family's behavior was similar to many of my friends' behavior toward me. Plenty of people couldn't even make eye contact or talk to me. They just didn't know what to say, and when they did talk, they didn't mention Russell or ask how I was doing. They seemed to think that by not mentioning him, the elephant would go away faster.

With my neighbors' children, I'd been there, on the other side of death. I knew how scary and awkward it was, so I was generous with my friends, willing to be the one to bridge the gap. Granted, I was grumpy about having to do it, but I did it. I made the effort, and I saw results.

With my family, I was stingier. I didn't *want* to bridge the gap. I wanted *them* to; I expected them to. They were my *family*, for goodness sake! How could they move on so fast? Hadn't they also lost a loved one—a grandson, a nephew, a cousin? Where were they now? How could they be back to normal without our Russell? How could they not even mention his name? His existence?

In their defense, my family was more than willing to help if I asked. My parents were fantastic about coming down to babysit the children whenever we needed them. They made themselves available at a moment's notice. My siblings seemed more than willing to talk—if *I* picked up the phone. I just hated having to ask, to pick up the phone. I wanted them to offer, to call.

I learned something visiting with my parents one day, five to six months after Russell's passing. I still was only speaking to them in monotone, trying in vain to hint at my utter despondency. We were there so the children could spend time with their grandparents. But I was still angry. I wore a heart-shaped necklace that said *Russell* on it, given to me by two thoughtful women who had also lost children.

Then my mom accidentally called Joey Russell.

It was the first time I'd heard her mention his name since the funeral. It was like music even though it was a mistake. Frantically, she looked at me, anxiety on her face as she tried to look for the words to undo the damage.

"I was looking at your necklace," she said recklessly, careful not to say Russell's name again. "And I must have read it when I was calling to Joey."

*Say it's okay,* I thought. *That I never hear Russell's name anymore, and it's nice to hear you say it. I want you to be comfortable talking about Russell. To know that I miss him so much and that remembering helps my pain.*

That's what my brain was telling my mouth to say, but my mouth was stubborn. I actually enjoyed watching my mom struggle, and I had the petty thought, *Serves you right.* I looked on, silent, knowing I was being selfish and mean. I'd been given the perfect opportunity to bridge the gap and make things better, just as I had with friends, but I hadn't done it. Instead I held on to the "mistakes" my mom had made those months. And that was my mistake.

Back at home, when I was able to reassess the situation, I felt bad. I felt more keenly that I had been given a gift, an open door, and I'd slammed it shut and walked away.

*This may be my future*, I realized: me uncomfortable and angry with my family, visiting only when I had to. Them just as uncomfortable as I was, everyone resorting to surface talk to avoid causing any pain. The only way I could be certain anything would change was if *I* changed it. I didn't know if my family would ever be comfortable enough to talk to me about Russell, and the only way I could be sure to have that conversation was to bring it up. I'd already missed one opportunity.

I wouldn't miss another.

I wasn't sure how to find one, so I did it as straightforwardly as possible. I called my older sister and tactlessly chewed her out for never calling to check on me. I told her how I felt, how disappointed and sad I was. With the ice broken, we had a nice conversation about Russell and my healing process. It was a relief to have a family member to talk to, and it chipped off a chunk of the anger I'd been carrying.

My sister took the conversation to heart and made a point to call often and ask how I was doing. We now share things on a much more personal level and have a closer relationship than ever before.

Later, I approached my dad. I wish I could say we had a calm exchange of ideas, but I can't. I yelled at him because I felt that because he was a therapist, he of all people should have known how much pain I was in. As I unloaded on him, he apologized profusely. He let me unload without arguing or defending himself. Ironically, that made me even angrier. I asked him to pass the information on to my mom. I just couldn't bear to hurt her like that.

She later called, and we talked about the situation civilly. They must have passed the word on to other family members because a few more siblings called to see how I was doing. But even today, some of my siblings still haven't called. They still don't talk about Russell.

That hurts.

I gave them all a copy of Russell's biography, with a note inside letting them know how much I yearn to talk about him. In most cases the book has opened the door and allowed us to talk comfortably about what I have been through and what I am going through.

My parents and some of my siblings have tried harder to keep in contact. I've taken a step in the right direction, and I've seen my family take a step there too.

A turning point for me came when my mom recognized my collection of heart rocks for what it was and gave me a heart-shaped piece of glass to add to it. Later, she gave me a Scooby-Doo candle. "When I saw it, it made me think of Russell," she said then suggested putting it on Russell's next birthday cake, if that was how we would be celebrating his next birthday.

My dad told me he had been thinking of Russell in the temple when my younger brother got married. He wondered if Russell would be there, and he felt a happy, confirming sensation that told him Russell was. I appreciated hearing that experience and felt grateful that my parents were becoming more comfortable talking to me about Russell.

I found out later that my interpretations and assumptions of my family members' actions had been terribly inaccurate. What I had interpreted as everyone "going back to normal" was actually everyone being steeped in their own grief. They didn't reach out to me because they were suffering as deeply as I was. What I interpreted as a lack of concern over my pain was actually the inability of my family members to express their own great sorrow and grief. They were unsure how to talk to me about it. They were afraid that the mere mention of Russell's name would cause more pain. Besides, it hurt *them* to talk about Russell.

What they didn't realize was how badly I craved hearing my little boy's name. I didn't realize it myself, not for a long time. I didn't realize how terrified I was of forgetting him. I had a hard time conjuring his image in my mind. The memories of him were no longer sharp and clear. Russell was so young that I assumed—wrongly again—that his friends and my friends would forget he'd ever even existed. That's why I was so sad and angry when it appeared that my family was forgetting him too.

In the end, I learned that we simply had had communication issues— which, unfortunately, are all too common after a tragic loss—and we all had different grieving styles. While I cried all the time and wrote and talked about my grief, my family grieved more introspectively—less talk and more thought helped them come to terms with the loss of their nephew and grandson. One family member has found it too painful and draining to wade through the grief and has had to back away from it. For him, talking and thinking too much about Russell is something he is simply not emotionally able to do yet.

As I finally shared my needs with my family, they became more open with their feelings, and in a real sense it validated Russell's life to me. It showed me that they had not forgotten, and it gave me a sense of security in knowing that they *will not* forget. Knowing that helped me to accept their silent grieving and to not take it personally.

When we at last felt more comfortable verbalizing our grief to each other, it felt to me like a wave of pent-up emotions was able to crash right out of my broken heart. With my anger and unresolved feelings gone, I now had room for love.

I still don't hear Russell's name as often as I would like, but I do hear it more than I used to. It sounds like the flutter of angels' wings. And though I never, ever tire of hearing it, for now, it is enough that I'm hearing it more.

* * *

It was our first fall without Russell, and my sister-in-law became pregnant with baby number four. I was struggling with not having a kindergartener and really, really wanted a baby to make up for my loss. I knew that we were done having children. Kirk and I had fasted and prayed after Joey was born, and we'd received the answer that our family was complete, but hormonally I wanted someone to fill the void left in our family. My arms hurt because Russell was not in them. I did not want a baby to have a spirit join our family—I wanted a replacement for Russell.

I'd been gypped out of future years of misshapen Mother's Day gifts, handprints to hang on the wall, homemade calendars. I still wanted these things. Joey was becoming too "big" for my kisses and hugs. I wanted a little child to love and to love me back. I wanted someone to sit on my lap when Joey wouldn't. In short, I wanted Russell back, and since I couldn't have that, I fantasized about having a new child.

While I was not in a happy place, I was working on being healthy. I had barely enough energy for me, my husband, and my children who were alive. I knew I didn't have enough for a pregnancy and a newborn. I *knew* that.

I could understand and accept all of that on an intellectual level, but emotionally I had days when I *yearned* to be pregnant. I wanted it to happen more than anything. I prayed for it, but I was always careful to add the caveat to help me be pregnant only if it would not affect my living kids' healing. I knew the answer was no even before asking but still found myself being irrationally hopeful. I was on an emotional roller coaster anyway and was now adding fuel to the fire with an illogical desire.

So when my sister-in-law, who had also previously announced she was done having kids, announced her pregnancy, I was upset. *Reacting this way is unfounded and absurd*, I told myself. But I couldn't feel happy for her. I felt almost betrayed by God. How could He give her a baby instead of me when we were both "done"? I didn't want to let my in-laws know about my crazy emotions, so I tried to analyze them as best I could. I wanted to have a handle on them so I wouldn't become bitter and resentful and possibly offensive. I knew that if I wasn't careful, I could lose the closeness I'd worked so hard to achieve with my Heavenly Father over the last year if I let my anger get out of hand.

*Of course I feel this way*, I rationalized. *It's only natural.*

Only natural. Just a few days before, I'd read about the natural man in the Book of Mormon. I'd never really understood what that passage meant— but now I was living it! For the first time, I really understood that some of my desires, although righteous and good, might cause emotions that were bad if left unchecked. I was jealous of my sister-in-law. If I wasn't careful, those natural feelings could turn ugly and vicious. I wasn't an enemy to God yet, but if I accepted my natural feelings and fed them more, I would be.

This realization helped me to be happy for my sister-in-law's fruitfulness. I was able to slowly loosen my grasp on my emotional desires and let the Lord be in charge again. Although my initial response pointed me in the wrong direction, correcting this mistake and recharting my course helped me better understand the scriptures and my human nature. Enough for me to let go and let God's will be the predominating factor in my life.

I know I'm not perfect and that I've made many mistakes through this grief process, but as I try to follow the Lord's will, I find I have the strength to do my best.

And I've found that to be enough.

# Chapter Twenty-One
## PERSPECTIVE

ABRAHAM LINCOLN ONCE SAID, "MOST folks are as happy as they make up their minds to be."[27] I think he was right in saying that *most* people are able to choose because there are times when it is impossible to do so. Abraham Lincoln was well acquainted with grief. He lost two children before his own premature death. He lived with his bereaved wife, who suffered from severe depression. I believe he was well aware of the line that divides those who *can* change their dispositions and those who *can't*.

Before Russell died, I'd experienced sadness and depression, but afterward, I realized I'd had no idea what those words really meant. I had decided as a teenager I wanted to be a relatively happy person, and for the most part, I was. Upsets and disappointments came, but they were fleeting. I could rise above them or get past them.

When Russell died, my whole world changed. I started at acceptance in the Kübler-Ross stages of grief. I mistakenly thought that since I knew it was God's will that Russell be taken back to his heavenly home, I would just run through the other stages without a backward glance. But logic can be completely and totally untrue.

There's a part of me that's sad all of the time. I can decide to get out of bed even though some mornings it can be a struggle. I can decide to talk and actively listen to my family. I can decide to be productive and fulfill as many of my motherly duties as I have the strength to.

But I can't seem to *decide* to be happy. I can have happy moments— and I enjoy them— but I can't seem to get rid of the gloom sitting heavy and oppressive on my chest.

My perspective has a great deal to do with how I feel about things. The way I view things colors my attitude about them, the way I feel toward them. I can get locked into a negative mindset because of incorrect assumptions.

Sometimes just changing my perspective helps me to change my attitude and feelings about a particular thing. When I struggle with emotions and feel besieged with problems, I try to analyze why. This helps me to put things into proper perspective and, hopefully, react in a healthier way.

In the hospital, when Russell lay dying on the operating table, I was given a beautiful perspective. I felt incredibly close to the Lord and basked in the overwhelming sensation of His love for me and my family. I saw the big picture in the Atonement and the plan of salvation. While I felt sad that Russell would be leaving us for a while, I felt that it would only be a while. It was almost as if I were up in heaven looking down. I could see everything. It all made sense, and it didn't seem like such a bad thing to bear. I could see that this would be a hard separation but that it was just for a short time. Russell was safe. He was in the celestial kingdom, graduating at the top of his class. With an eternal perspective, I knew there were worse "deaths" I could go through—the death of a marriage or the spiritual death of a loved one.

Then reality took over. Living each day that I spent immersed in grief wore down my reserves and frayed my nerves. It got harder to see the big picture. Instead, I found myself confined to this earth and questioning all the recent events in my life. It no longer felt like we'd be together with Russell in a while. It felt like an eternity. Each day without Russell made him seem farther away.

When I felt like some of my memories of Russell were beginning to fade, it broke my heart all over again. Being mortal is hard. We live on mortal time through the hours and years. Every step I made took me one step away from the time I'd last been with my son. Every minute that ticked on was one minute longer since the last time I'd seen him.

During a Relief Society lesson about the life of Emma Smith, the teacher talked about Emma's life after her beloved husband, Joseph, had been brutally assassinated. Emma remarried a man who, by his own account, was not religious. He was said to be abusive when he drank. Women had few rights at the time, and some in our Relief Society wondered if remarrying had really been Emma's choice. She lived the best she could, helping many people in her community. She was charitable and generous, not only with money but also with her time and talents. When Emma's new husband told her he had fathered a child outside of their marriage, Emma invited the woman and her child into their home and took care of them.[28]

The Relief Society teacher then said that Emma Smith was truly blessed because she was able to live such a long life.

I sat there thinking otherwise. My perspective was different. I couldn't help but wonder if, after Joseph was killed, Emma wanted to die too. I wondered if she often felt her longevity was more of a curse than a blessing. I wondered if she asked God why He wouldn't let her die too and be with all the children she'd lost and with the husband she loved. I wondered if the pain wore her down. I wondered if I would have the nerve to ask her these questions when I met her.

No matter how she felt, I admire the way she continued to live her life. She is a great example to me, especially during those times when I am impatient to see Russell and am tired of waiting.

I still try to "look down" on this experience with an eternal perspective, and sometimes it helps. But sometimes I am too angry or too tired to do anything but look around at the mess. I've felt that Russell is behind me and that I have no choice but to "walk away" from him and our time together. It hurts me to view my life like that, to feel helpless while time drags me further away from my son. However, in looking at it from a different perspective, I've realized that every step I take and every minute that ticks on brings me closer to my death and my eventual reunion with Russell. Although I don't anticipate that time to come soon, I now like to visualize myself walking *toward* Russell rather than away from him.

One of the things that has been hardest for me to change my perspective about is ambulances and sirens. Just the sight or sound sends a chill down my spine and brings me back to the emergency room and harrows up my anxieties. My throat closes up, and I have a hard time breathing. My heart either skips a beat or races out of control. I keep telling myself that it's good to see an ambulance speeding down the street. It's rushing to help someone. Perhaps a person will be saved.

That's what my conscious mind says. But now that I know happy outcomes aren't always the case, I can't help but think, *Someone's life is changing, and they have no idea how bad it is going to be.*

No matter what I consciously try to tell myself, it doesn't help because I know the truth. And at the sound of a siren, I imagine what someone else is experiencing. Strangely, I don't think much of the person in trouble— although I say a quick prayer for them. My mind is focused on the family of the injured person. How will they get through this? How will they cope with the loss? I say a longer prayer for them because I know all too well the pain and anguish they might face.

How do I change my perspective on this? I'm not sure if I can. When I see or hear an ambulance, I'm not as apprehensive or afraid as I once was.

My body doesn't immediately react with a panic attack as it once did. But I can't seem to stop my emotional concerns for the injured person's family.

I pray that the family will have the strength to accept and live through whatever terrors they're confronted with. That's all I can do. Then I have to let it go.

I have found that my grief ebbs and flows like the waves on a beach. Some days I feel good—almost normal. I can smile and laugh even when thinking about Russell. I can appreciate the lessons I have learned from his death. I can reach out to try and lift others. I have energy, and in many ways, I feel renewed. Then a wave of despair comes crashing down, and I'm pulled into deep water. I flail around, more than sad. I'm downhearted and low. My chest hurts. My heart hurts. Once again, it hurts to breathe.

These sad times come around with no warning or reason. What to do about these emotions? These are times when choosing to be happy seems preposterous and downright impossible. I have ridden out these tough times, sometimes giving in to the despair and crying for days on end, sometimes trying to fake it till I make it.

A friend well acquainted with death told me something once that changed my perspective of these miserable and dispirited times. He thinks he feels this way because, at those melancholy times, perhaps his deceased wife's spirit is close by and his spirit can recognize it. He thinks his body reacts in a depressed manner because of the closeness he can't physically feel—it's physically painful to be so close and yet still so far away.

I like this idea. When I struggle to breathe and to move, I like to think that Russell is extra close. Just imagining that helps motivate me to get up and move. It is the perspective I need to help me survive those difficult times.

As I've mentioned, the scriptures seem so different to me now. I feel my Heavenly Father talking directly to *me* when I read a particularly moving passage.

This first happened around eight months after Russell died, when I was reading the New Testament, in John 6, where Jesus miraculously feeds five thousand with a few loaves of bread and two small fish. The next day, the people seek Jesus because they want more food. Jesus, seeing their superficial esteem, tries harder to show them His true purpose as He gives them His bread of life sermon. "*I* am the bread of life: he that cometh to me shall never hunger; and he that believeth on me shall never thirst."[29] Jesus continues to share with His followers the reason for His existence. He tells them quite plainly that He will be giving up His flesh and His blood to bring eternal life to those who truly follow Him.

This was a hard saying for many to hear. Unfortunately some were offended and chose to stop following Jesus. In verse 66, some of Christ's disciples were among the group that left. Seeing His friends leaving must have been painful for the Savior. He turned to the Twelve and asked them poignantly in verse 67, "Will ye also go away?"

Russell's death was a hard pill to swallow. Christ was there, and yet His hand was stayed from saving my son. I also had a decision to make. When I read these verses, I felt the weight of the question "Will ye also go away?"

I know many who have become angry with God for allowing their loved ones to die, for allowing their lives to become empty and sad. For not filling the void or covering the abyss.

Would I also turn and leave? I could, but then I would be left with so much less. No. My answer is like that of Peter, when he said, "Lord, to whom would we go? thou hast the words of eternal life."[30]

God has allowed me to go through a painful experience. He did not save me from it. Instead, He held my hand and walked me through it. And because He allowed His own Son to die, my son will live on eternally. And so will I, with my son and the rest of my family. How can I leave? No, I will hold fast to my Heavenly Father, my Savior, and the truths of the gospel. In my blackest night, in my bleakest hour, through my tears and during my loneliest days, I remember that Jesus Christ has the words of eternal life. And that gives me the greatest perspective of all.

# Chapter Twenty-Two
## GIFTS

IN THEIR OWN WAYS, EACH member of our family was struck down and broken when Russell died. As we tried picking up the pieces to put them back together, they didn't seem to fit anymore. We've each had to heal and rebuild ourselves, and that has taken time. A traumatic loss has the potential to tear down and rip apart. But we wanted to be united, not isolated and alone. Each of us has brought gifts to the table that have helped in our healing. These gifts have had the ability to meld and intertwine our lives to make them more connected and stronger than ever.

Kirk's gift is for building unity through adventure. We've gone on thousands of camping trips all over the Western United States, kayaking adventures, hikes of varying lengths and terrains, road trips, bike treks, rock climbing escapades—you name it, we've probably done it or would like to do it.

When Kirk asked me out on our first date, he didn't take me to some sissy movie or a fancy dinner. Kirk took me rock climbing, and it was *awesome*! Climbing a thousand feet up a rock face is at once scary and exhilarating. I had to trust myself, my shoes, the rope, and Kirk. Luckily, we were already good friends. I knew what a true-blue person he was, so trust came easily. Kirk proposed on the top of our favorite rock-climbing mountain and invited me to continue our adventures into eternity. I readily accepted. And I have never been let down.

When Russell died, I wanted to freeze for a while so I could come to terms with my new life, but of course life kept on moving away from me. I tried in vain to keep up. If I'd had my way, I would have stopped the earth from spinning on its axis, just for a month or two! Just until I felt like I could wrap my mind around all the events of the past few days.

Kirk would have none of it. He planned a camping trip for us within those first few weeks after the funeral. I was sad to go camping without Russell. It seemed so lonely, but off we went.

And we enjoyed it.

It wasn't as happy and carefree an adventure as it used to be, but the trip wasn't as bad as I expected either. Then we went on the road trip to Death Valley, and I began finding the heart rocks.

As time went on, I began having meaningful experiences with the Lord and with Russell. I felt them both close, watching over our little family. Kirk and the children and I were enjoying each other's company as we learned to enjoy life again.

Just as I was compelled to write the Russell book, Kirk was compelled to create adventures for us. We went on more trips than usual that year. Every major holiday except Christmas found us in a new location, away from the sadness of home. It helped our family regroup and get used to our new dynamic. Taking short trips away made my life bearable. I found it was easier to breathe away from home. The trips lessened the weight of all the "firsts" without Russell.

Kirk came up with our family motto based on the scripture "Except the Lord build the house, they labour in vain that build it."[31] Our family values became serve God, family first, work hard, be kind, tell the truth, and be adventurous.

I did not feel adventurous. I felt cautious and afraid. I was willing to go along for the ride, but I wouldn't step out on my own. Kirk's gift to the family kept us moving forward, kept us brave.

* * *

Russell loved music. He would sit in the backseat of the van, look out the window, and yell to me, "Turn on the radio to a daddy song!" That meant a song with a male singer. If a female singer came on, Russell yelled, "Skip!" until I came to an appropriate song. Then he looked out the window again, tapping his feet to the beat and loudly singing what he thought were the lyrics. I looked at him in the rearview mirror often and now have that picture of him forever etched in my mind.

After Russell died, I couldn't bear to turn on the radio. Hearing "daddy songs" he'd liked—and mommy songs he didn't—was too gut wrenching. I couldn't stand the fast, bouncy rhythm of happy songs. And the sad songs . . . they usually dealt with the loss of a loved one, usually in the form of a breakup, but all I could hear in them was, "My little boy is gone."

My normally noisy, happy life was suddenly turned off and replaced by a hollow silence that echoed loudly in my head, reverberating through my brain and shaking my broken heart. If I did listen to music, it was subdued, mellow, sad. Such music fed my mood and kept my spirits low.

Then, about a year after Russell died, Karissa became a teenager and discovered music. Suddenly our house became vibrant and alive, thumping with a beat and accompanied by a voice. We were lucky that Karissa enjoyed only appropriate rock songs and turned off any with swearing or questionable lyrics.

But our house was filled with music again!

Sometimes I found the music too loud or overwhelming. But still, it awoke something inside me I thought had died with Russell. I now had happy songs in my head to confront the nightmares that had taken refuge there. My life became a little less heavy when I found myself tapping my toes to a beat and humming along. I found I could smile more, and sometimes I could even sing along.

I still don't turn on the radio when I'm alone at home or in the car— it's still too hard without Russell's little voice in the backseat requesting a "daddy song." But being alone in the silence isn't as deafening or suffocating as it used to be. I can reflect and ponder, talk to the Lord, and think. And I know when Karissa joins me on a ride, she will be giving me her gift.

\* \* \*

Because I'm not very organized, we are late to many things, and sometimes, even when we are on time, I've forgotten to bring something important from home. Kyle is very organized. He likes his room clean. He does his homework right away and finishes projects long before they're due. A long time ago, Kyle learned that there are benefits to being early. If he is early to school, he gets to play on the playground. If he is early to Scouts, chances are he'll be in charge of the flag ceremony. If he's early to church, he gets to talk to any friends who are also early. Kyle has taught Jake the benefits of being early, and now Jake tries to be early too.

Kyle learned through experience that if he helps me get children in the car or gather the necessary items for an activity, it increases our chances of being early or at least being on time. Kyle tends to be most helpful when we're going places that he is eager to be early to.

After Russell died, everything was hard; I had to concentrate to remember how to get dressed. I often forgot to brush my teeth or do my hair. Or I just didn't care or see the point of doing those things. Being on time didn't matter anymore. Even showing up fell low on my list of priorities. I could barely motivate myself, let alone find the energy and the strength to motivate my children. Without Kyle, a lot of things would have slid.

He kept us organized. He reminded me when it was Scouts. He gave me advanced warning when his school play was on the horizon. He let me know when we needed to hurry because we were running late. I found I had the strength I needed because I could see how important my being strong was to Kyle and to the other kids.

At a time when I just wanted to go back to bed and forget the world was moving forward, Kyle kept me moving. I hate to think what would have happened if I hadn't kept moving. If I'd stopped, I doubt I could have started again. At least for a long, long time. Kyle helped us keep that forward momentum. He kept us on track.

\* \* \*

We love to laugh together as a family. We tell jokes, we tell funny stories, we look for the humor in our day and then share it with each other. After Russell died, I could barely smile. There were happy moments, but they were fleeting. It seemed that all the colors had faded. Nothing was beautiful or interesting or even funny. I could not laugh, nor could I think of ways to make others laugh. Russell had just been learning how to tell knock-knock jokes. Even though they made little sense, they still made me laugh. Now I felt as if all of the joy had been sucked out of my life.

As Russell's best friend, Jake spent hours just laughing with his brother. A sensitive Jake missed those moments with Russell and tried to re-create them for us. Jake held on to his smile. Sure, at times Jake cried, but he could also bring the laughter back to our house.

Jake told jokes, most of them made up himself. Some made absolutely no sense, but that made us laugh even harder. Jake pulled practical jokes on us. Again, some made us laugh more than others. He got dressed in funny outfits and walked around the house acting as if nothing was out of the ordinary. He loved getting a reaction, loved to see what it would take to get one.

In a time when we were all crying, Jake helped us to remember to laugh.

\* \* \*

When Russell died, I lost the magic. I had no desire to go up in the attic and bring boxes down for special holidays or to keep up our family traditions.

Larry the leprechaun came in March and brought some of Russell's favorite candy and a note to say how sorry he was that Russell was no longer with us. The school fairy came, but she cried as she set out school supplies for everyone *except* the boy who would have been in kindergarten. The tooth fairy had to be reminded a few times to leave some money and take the tooth.

When Easter came that first year, all those bunnies and eggs waiting to come down out of the attic were vile and offensive to me. What did they have to do with the glorious gift of the Resurrection? They were now so meaningless, so insignificant when compared to the Atonement of my Savior. I felt if I put up those decorations, it would almost be an affront to God. So they stayed in the attic collecting dust. Instead, I put out the one picture I have of the Garden Tomb in Israel.

Christmas was the same. The fat, jolly Santas I saw everywhere infuriated me. How in the world could they be so happy? How could Santa promise to give me or my family a special Christmas wish? How could he compare to the Christ child, lying in a manger, full of hope and promise? It was upsetting—even insulting—to see Santa everywhere and to hardly see Christ anywhere. Besides, the older children knew the truth about Santa, so I didn't feel like I needed to pretend anymore. Santa didn't even really need to come to our house. Of course, he still did, but he did it grudgingly that first year.

The other holidays—Halloween, Thanksgiving, Valentine's Day, and others—were bad, but their decorations and traditions didn't seem as odious. I still didn't decorate in my usual style. I became a minimalist—only putting up the most cherished pieces.

I felt no magic.

Santa still scared Joey. He didn't care who left the Easter eggs as long as they had candy in them. The candy part of Halloween was great, but he was leery of the costumes. Joey didn't seem to notice that the magic was gone that first year.

That second year, though, things changed. Joey began to dress up in Russell's old costumes after Halloween. He began wearing costumes daily, sometimes changing several times a day. It reminded me of Russell, who dressed up just as often.

I never encouraged it in Joey, but I never discouraged it either. I tried not to compare Joey with Russell or even mention that they had been Russell's costumes first. One day I was trying to get Joey to wear some regular clothes for a Cub Scout pack meeting. Instead, he decided to wear a Spiderman suit with a Superman hat and an orange cape.

When I tried harder to get Joey to change, he said, "But Mom, Russell wants me to wear *this*."

Much to the amusement of all, Joey wore the whole wild ensemble to pack meeting.

Somehow, that Christmas, Joey learned about Santa Claus. He was thrilled at the mystery of it all—the elves, the flying reindeer, how Santa could sneak into the house without us hearing, and, of course, the toys. Joey couldn't get enough. We read every book we had and went to the library for more. Joey wanted to see all of the decorations. He wanted us to get the tree on December 1 so we could decorate it and have it up all month. He was so excited that a little of the sparkle rubbed off on us. We began to be excited too. We listened to Christmas music. We sang it. We made Christmas goodies and passed them out. We ate the goodies passed on to us. We looked for elves, and we acted like elves as we did secret surprises for others.

Joey was awestruck with the little baby in the manger. He was captivated by the story of Jesus, and he seemed to understand how meaningful and important this little person was. Joey delighted in each and every detail. His thrill at every new aspect was contagious, and I found myself getting caught up in it. Joey helped us to understand once again that the magic of Christmas was not just found in Santa but in the whole season, every part of it. That year, Joey gave us his gift for Christmas, the gift of magic and wonder.

\* \* \*

I think Russell's gift to us was the best. Before he died, I thought I had a good understanding of the plan of salvation. I thought I understood about my Heavenly Father's love for His children. I was aiming to make it to the highest kingdom—one so celestial and magnificent that families are able to remain united for all eternity. That was my goal. But I was never quite sure if I would be good enough for it, if my works would qualify me for exaltation. It seemed so far away—a vague and intangible reality. I knew it existed, but it existed like a cloud in my understanding. I couldn't touch it. I couldn't even see it properly because it tended to fade like a mist before my view. The distance between heaven and me was staggering.

When Russell lay dying in the hospital, his spirit did something amazing. He tied an unbreakable silver cord (made out of moonbeams maybe?) from heaven to earth. As the hosts of heaven and Jesus and Heavenly Father came down to meet Russell, we were brought up halfway to meet them. I can't describe in words how beautiful, how sacred, how *heavenly* it was when we said good-bye to Russell. It was heartbreaking, but for a brief moment, I was graciously allowed to peer into heaven and experience its goodness. I saw how fleeting this time on earth really was. I knew that I would see Russell again, and soon. I felt the goodness, the light, the love that exists there.

And it felt *familiar*. It felt like I was at home. And I knew with a perfect understanding at the time that I would be able to one day return.

Our family now has a new reason to choose the right and follow Jesus. We have a new reason to look to the heavens. Now we *belong* to heaven. We know someone there, someone who is preparing our home and awaiting our arrival, someone who showed us that the death of a righteous person is not sad for that person even though it is excruciating for those left behind. That was Russell's gift to us. By going there first, he made heaven a real place, a place where we will be able to live together. In his own special way, Russell connected us to heaven with a bond that can never be broken.

## Chapter Twenty-Three
### LOOKING BACK

ON ONE PARTICULAR FAMILY RUN/bike ride about a year and a half after Russell's death, we followed the Aliso Creek Trail for a few miles as it meandered through parks and soccer fields and past housing developments. Since this was my first time down this stretch of the trail, I had much to see—much more than I could even take in. I noticed bushes and flowers, playgrounds that might be fun to visit later, and lots of rocks on the side of the trail. Yes, I was on the lookout for heart-shaped ones.

After a few miles, we turned to head back to the car. I was still looking at the same scenery, but the new perspective and the fact that I had seen it all before changed what I saw.

The first thing I noticed this time were the Saddleback Mountains. They'd been at my back for the first leg of the run, but now they towered over me. Maybe because I was now looking heavenward, I noticed birds flying through majestic clouds. I saw the same playgrounds and soccer fields, but now my eyes were drawn upward to the bluffs. What had been mundane scenery suddenly became beautiful and striking. I could see so much more by revisiting this place as I changed my direction and perspective.

I think this is why I like to be introspective. I have found that revisiting experiences later sometimes gives me a different perspective of them. I like to mull things over in my mind, turn them around in my brain. There is only so much "scenery" from an experience I can take in the first time around. By going back in my mind to past experiences, I can usually pick out new information; I can see the Lord's hand working in ways I hadn't noticed before. Even through painful memories—or perhaps *especially* through painful memories—I can see how prayers were answered, prayers I hadn't verbally expressed or realized I was asking. I can better see the beauty in the sorrow.

Some of life's experiences are too painful to revisit for a while, and Russell's death was no exception. But I was blessed to be able to see the hand of the Lord in our lives during the whole experience. I knew He was there, and while I knew there was more to uncover, it was too raw for a long time. Too exquisite. I didn't want to forget details, so I wrote everything down. I wrote haphazardly, straight through the experience without stopping to ponder or reflect on it. If I let the emotion of what had happened get the best of me, I wouldn't have been able to record the facts.

After writing, I shut my journal and put that experience on a shelf as far from my conscious mind as I could. Of course, those who have lived through great loss know there's only so far one can be distanced from it.

I only dealt with what I had to. I knew one day I'd be able to take everything out and look at it. One day I could revisit the experiences and the pain would not be as acute. So I did what I could and decided not to worry about what I couldn't. The time would come.

That time *did* come. This book is ample evidence of that. I've written for me, as a way to document my travels back into the abyss and to show myself that there is a way out. I've written for my family so they can know the feelings of my heart I struggle to express verbally. I want them to know of my trust and dependence on the Lord's plan, that even though we travel down painful roads, the Lord is at our side. Sometimes we can't see Him or feel Him, but He is still there. Sometimes we know He's there, but we hurt anyway. Sometimes we see Him beside us, but we're still wounded and injured. His love for us is complete and unconditional, even if He doesn't give us the respite we desire. His ability to heal our wounded spirits is limitless, even though His time line for healing is not the same as ours.

I find it vital to sometimes turn around and wander back up a path I have already traveled. The more times I reflect on my experiences, the more reassurances I have that He was there. The small, seemingly insignificant, commonplace happenings in my life take on a new and deeper magnitude when I look again through different eyes.

I know that this painful time of my life is just that—a time of my life. The lessons I have learned through this particular era have spanned the years now. Looking back, I remember lessons I'd forgotten. They have been stepping stones, helping me learn and prepare as I gradually move forward.

Later, I will see how my "Russell lessons" prepared me for what is to come. I like to think that the death of my son is the hardest thing I'll ever have to endure, but I worry that these lessons are designed to make me stronger for other trials that will follow. I don't know.

All I know, all I have learned throughout my life, is that my Heavenly Father is real. He loves me with the sweet, unconditional, fierce love of a parent. Jesus Christ truly walked the earth and saved us all through His Atonement. They both know me and are walking by my side, giving me the knowledge and the help I need. They will carry me when I'm too weak to continue, or they will send angels, from the living and the dead, to bolster me and give me the strength I lack. Looking back on my life has shown me the mercy and love of my Heavenly family, and it has given me the courage to turn and walk forward. I know with Their help, I will eventually overcome all and join them again, just beyond the veil.

Just Beyond the Veil

You left us all so suddenly
You eternally set sail,
But we know where your soul lives now
Just beyond the veil.

Sometimes you seem so far away
And my aching heart begins to fail,
But then I seem to sense you watching
Just beyond the veil.

When the storms rage all around me
And the winds begin to gale,
You whisper peace and guidance from
Just beyond the veil.

Sometimes I feel so close to you,
Your love fastened with a nail.
That's when I see you smile at me
Just beyond the veil.

I know we'll be together;
In this I shall prevail.
Just try to wipe my big, fat, wet, sloppy girl kisses off
When we again embrace
Just beyond the veil.

## *Epilogue*

I GUESS THIS IS THE lesson I've tried to convey: we have the opportunity to learn when we struggle through trials and hard times, whether these trials and hard times are deserved or not. Yes, this life is hard, and it is often unfair. That is why it isn't forever. Our Heavenly Father loves us like a father because he is *our* Father. He knows each of us personally and loves us even more than we love our children. Because of this, He prepared a plan for us. This plan required us to leave His presence and come to earth. While here, we need to rely on our faith in Him and His goodness. Even when bad things happen. Especially when bad things happen.

He is accessible through prayer and meditation so that anyone, no matter how evil or unbelieving, can find the answers by simply asking and really listening. What we do with those answers demonstrates our level of faith and belief. This life is a test, and it is fraught with uncertainties and unspeakable pain. But again, it is not forever.

How could God let bad things happen? Because He has so much more to offer on the other side of the veil. When our memories are returned of our pre-earth life with God and we compare our actions here on earth with the glorious life we will have on the other side, all things will be made clear. Then we will overwhelmingly agree on the goodness of God. Then we will see how the pain, the sorrow, and the anguish fit like a puzzle to teach us and prepare us to live with our wonderful, loving, amazing Creator. Then it will all fit and make sense, and we will rejoice.

I may feel embarrassed and unprotected out here, bearing my soul like this to anyone who will listen. But how can I keep it inside, hidden, when it is such glorious news? I want to shout it from the housetops! We will live again! We will see our loved ones again—hold them and squeeze them and love them! God will "wipe away all tears from their eyes; and there shall be no more death, neither sorrow, nor crying, neither shall there be any more pain."[32] We will then see clearly the beauty that will be ours for eternity. Christ has overcome the world for us, and one day, we will overcome it too. Our loved ones who have passed on have already overcome it. They are waiting for us, just beyond the veil. If I am really quiet and I really listen, sometimes I can even hear them laughing for joy.

# Additional Books on Grief and Loss

DeVita-Raeburn, Elizabeth. *The Empty Room: Surviving the Loss of a Brother or Sister at Any Age.* New York: Scribner, 2004.

Emswiler, Mary Ann. *Guiding Your Child Through Grief.* New York: Bantam Books, 2000.

James, John W. *When Children Grieve: For Adults to Help Children Deal with Death, Divorce, Pet Loss, Moving, and Other Losses.* New York: HarperCollins, 2001.

Mehren, Elizabeth. *After the Darkest Hour the Sun Will Shine Again: A Parent's Guide to Coping with the Loss of a Child.* New York City: Simon & Schuster, 1997.

O'Hara, Kathleen A. *A Grief like No Other: Surviving the Violent Death of Someone You Love.* New York: Marlow & Co., 2006.

Schiraldi, Glenn R. *The Post-traumatic Stress Disorder Sourcebook: A Guide to Healing, Recovery, and Growth,* 2nd ed. New York: McGraw Hill, 2009.

# Endnotes

1   Daniel 3:17–18, emphasis added.

2   See Luke 8:49–56.

3   *Ensign*, November 2002.

4   *Ensign*, May 2004.

5   See Logue, Christopher, "Come to the Edge," http://poemof-theday.blogspot.com.

6   1 Peter 1:7.

7   "To the Women of the Church," *Ensign*, November 2003.

8   *Ensign*, May 2005.

9   "Seek Ye the Kingdom of God," *Ensign*, May 2006.

10   *Hymns*, no. 3.

11   *Hymns*, no. 85.

12   *Teachings of the Presidents of the Church: Joseph Smith*, 174.

13   Ibid, 176.

14   Ibid, 177.

15   Matthew 5:4.

16   Alma 29:1–2, emphasis added.

17   3 Nephi 28:9, emphasis added.

18   See "Washed Clean," *Ensign*, November 1986.

19   See D&C 38:30.

20   See Philippians 4:7.

21   "None Were with Him," *Ensign*, May 2009.

22   John 16:32, emphasis added.

23    Matthew 27:46, emphasis added.

24    Callister, Tad R., *The Infinite Atonement* (Salt Lake City: Deseret Book Company, 2000), 114.

25    1 Nephi 11:17.

26    Proverbs 3:5–6.

27    http://lifechangequotes.com/abraham-lincoln-happy-quote/.

28    See Youngreen, Buddy, *Reflections of Emma* (Provo: Maasai, Inc., 2001), 42.

29    John 6:35, emphasis added.

30    John 6:68.

31    Psalm 127:1.

32    Revelation 21:4.

## About the Author

JENNY HESS WAS BORN IN Boston, Massachusetts. She is an avid quilter and loves the outdoors. After serving a mission in Denmark, Jenny graduated from California State University, Long Beach, where she met her husband, Kirk. They have five kids—four living on earth and one living in heaven. As a family, they love spending time together camping, hiking, biking, exploring, and rock climbing. Jenny's story can be found on Mormon.org. A video vignette detailing how the scriptures helped heal her is currently being shown at the Los Angeles Temple Visitors' Center in California.